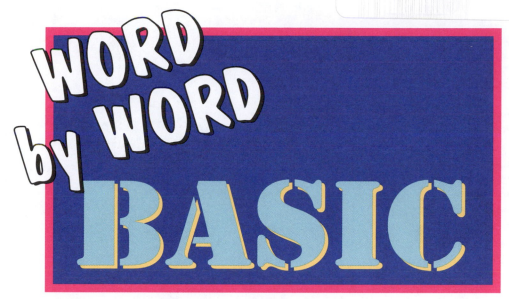

WORD by WORD BASIC

Literacy Workbook

Steven J. Molinsky · Bill Bliss

Contributing Authors
Dorothy Almanza
Deborah L. Schaffer
Carol H. Van Duzer

PRENTICE HALL REGENTS
Upper Saddle River, New Jersey 07458

Publisher: *Mary Jane Peluso*
AVP / Director of Production and Manufacturing: *Aliza Greenblatt*
Executive Managing Editor: *Dominick Mosco*
Electronic Production and Page Composition: *Wendy Wolf*
Electronic Production Specialists: *Carey Davies and Steven Greydanus*
Art Director / Cover Design: *Merle Krumper*
Interior Design: *Kenny Beck and Wendy Wolf*
Manufacturing Manager: *Ray Keating*
Pre-formatter: *Rose Ann Merrey*

Illustrations: *Richard E. Hill*

The authors gratefully acknowledge the contribution of Tina Carver
in the development of the *Word by Word* program.

© 1999 by PRENTICE HALL REGENTS
Prentice-Hall, Inc.
Upper Saddle River, New Jersey 07458

Printed in the United States of America

10   9   8   7   6   5   4   3   2   1

ISBN 0-13-278524-2

Prentice-Hall International (UK) Limited, *London*
Prentice-Hall of Australia Pty. Limited, *Sydney*
Prentice-Hall Canada Inc., *Toronto*
Prentice-Hall Hispanoamericana, S.A., *Mexico*
Prentice-Hall of India Private Limited, *New Delhi*
Prentice-Hall of Japan, Inc., *Tokyo*
Simon & Schuster Asia Pte. Ltd., *Singapore*
Editora Prentice-Hall do Brasil, Ltda., *Rio de Janeiro*

CONTENTS

A. CIRCLE THE SAME WORD

1.	NAME	STREET	NUMBER	(NAME)	STATE
2.	CITY	STATE	ADDRESS	CITY	LAST
3.	ADDRESS	ADDRESS	NAME	NUMBER	CITY
4.	STATE	STREET	FIRST	LAST	STATE
5.	STREET	FIRST	STATE	STREET	LAST

B. MATCHING

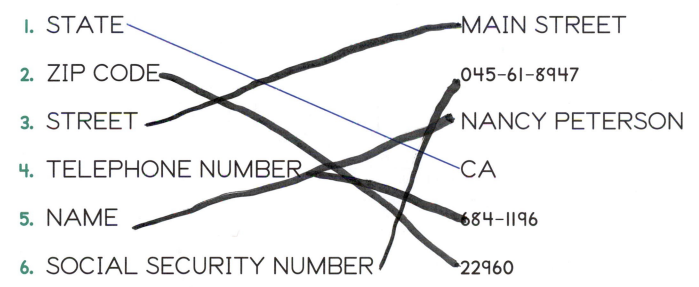

1. STATE   MAIN STREET

2. ZIP CODE   045-61-8947

3. STREET   NANCY PETERSON

4. TELEPHONE NUMBER   CA

5. NAME   684-1196

6. SOCIAL SECURITY NUMBER   22960

ABCDEFGHIJKLMNOPQR

C. FILL OUT THE FORM

NAME: _____
          FIRST   LAST

ADDRESS: _____
          NUMBER   STREET   APT.

          _____
          CITY   STATE   ZIP CODE

TELEPHONE NUMBER: _____

SOCIAL SECURITY NUMBER: _____

D. FILL OUT THE FORM

NAME
FIRST   LAST

ADDRESS
NUMBER   STREET   APT.

CITY   STATE   ZIP CODE

TELEPHONE NUMBER

SOCIAL SECURITY NUMBER

S T U V W X Y Z 0 1 2 3 4 5 6 7 8 9

E.   INTERVIEW

Talk to three people. Write the information.

<table>
<tr><td>Name</td><td>Telephone Number</td></tr>
<tr><td>1. _____</td><td>_____</td></tr>
<tr><td>2. _____</td><td>_____</td></tr>
<tr><td>3. _____</td><td>_____</td></tr>
</table>

F.   LISTENING

Listen and circle the words you hear.

1. (name)
   address

2. zip code
   apartment number

3. telephone
   social security

4. state
   street

5. middle
   city

6. first
   last

G.   JOURNAL

My first name is _____.

My last name is _____.

My address is _____.

My telephone number is _____.

A.   WHO ARE THEY?

1. grandmother   <u>b</u>

2. son   _____

3. father   _____

4. daughter   _____

5. mother   _____

6. grandfather   _____

B.   MATCHING

1. FATHER   sister

2. SISTER   mother

3. BROTHER   daughter

4. MOTHER   father

5. SON   brother

6. DAUGHTER   son

Aa Bb Cc Dd Ee Ff Gg Hh Ii Jj Kk Ll Mm

C. WHAT'S MISSING?

1. w_i_fe
   s__ster

2. fathe__
   mothe__

3. hu__band
   __on

4. grands__n
   br__ther

5. b__by
   d__ughter

6. grandmo____er
   grandfa____er

D. WHICH GROUP?

daughter	father	son	wife
husband	brother	sister	mother

Parents

Children

1. _f_ _a_ _t_ _h_ _e_ _r_

2. _m_ _ _ _ _ _

3. _h_ _ _ _ _ _ _

4. _w_ _ _ _

5. _s_ _ _

6. _d_ _ _ _ _ _ _

7. _b_ _ _ _ _ _ _

8. _s_ _ _ _ _ _

Nn Oo Pp Qq Rr Ss Tt Uu Vv Ww Xx Yy Zz

A. WHO ARE THEY?

1.	nephew	<u>d</u>
2.	aunt	___
3.	niece	___
4.	cousin	___
5.	uncle	___

B. WHAT'S MISSING?

1. a <u>u</u> n t

    _ n c l e

2. _ e p h e w

    _ i e c e

3. c _ _ u s i n

    s _ n – i n – l a w

4. s i s t _ _ – i n – l a w

    b _ o t h _ _ – i n – l a w

C. WHICH GROUP?

aunt	cousin	nephew	niece	uncle

n e p h e w   c _ _ _ _ _   a _ _ _

u _ _ _ _   n _ _ _ _

D. WHO ARE THEY?

aunt	uncle

father	aunt

1. He's my _____ uncle _____ .

5. He's my _____ .

2. She's my _____ .

6. She's my _____ .

nephew	niece

sister	uncle

3. He's my _____ .

7. He's my _____ .

4. She's my _____ .

8. She's my _____ .

E. JOURNAL

This is my family.

My _____ 's name is _____ .

My _____ 's name is _____ .

My _____ 's name is _____ .

A. MATCHING

1.

2.

3.

4.

5.

6.

take a bath

brush my teeth

comb my hair

get up

take a shower

go to bed

WHAT DO YOU DO EVERY DAY?

brush	eat	make	shave	sleep	wash

1. I _____make_____ breakfast.

2. I _____ my hair.

3. I _____ my face.

4. I _____ dinner.

5. I _____.

6. I _____.

C. LISTENING

Listen. Write the correct number.

___ take a shower   ___ make dinner

___ brush teeth   ___ shave

_1_ take a bath

EVERYDAY ACTIVITIES II

A. LISTENING

Listen. Put a check under the correct picture.

1. ___✓___ _____   2. _____ _____

3. _____ _____   4. _____ _____

5. _____ _____   6. _____ _____

B. MATCHING

1. wash   TV

2. play   the dishes

3. watch   the cat

4. feed   basketball

C. WHAT DO YOU DO EVERY DAY?

dust	study	vacuum	play	watch TV	exercise

1. I _____study_____.　2. I _____.　3. I _____.

4. I _____.　5. I _____.　6. I _____.

D. LISTENING

Listen. Write the correct number.

___ sweep   ___ wash the dishes

___ vacuum   ___ do the laundry

_1_ exercise   ___ play basketball

E. JOURNAL

Every day I _____, I _____,

I _____, and I _____.

A. WHAT'S THE WORD?

teacher	student	board	desk	book
pencil	clock	ruler	notebook	map

a. _____clock_____

b. _____

c. _____

d. _____

e. _____

f. _____

g. _____

h. _____

i. _____

j. _____

B. LISTENING

Listen and circle the word you hear.

1. pen   (pencil)   4. eraser   ruler

2. pencil   paper   5. notebook   textbook

3. chalk   clock   6. computer   calculator

C. WHAT'S IN THE CLASSROOM?

Look at page 12 of the dictionary. Write the correct word.

| map   book   clock   computer   globe |

1. The c l o c k is next to the flag.

2. The g _ _ _ _ is on the bookshelf.

3. The b _ _ _ is on the teacher's desk.

4. The m _ _ is next to the bulletin board.

5. The _ _ _ _ _ _ _ _ is next to the TV.

D. JOURNAL

In my classroom there is _____

_____

_____ .

A. LISTENING

Listen. Put a check under the correct picture.

1. ✔ _____ _____ **2.** _____ _____

3. _____ _____ **4.** _____ _____

5. _____ _____ **6.** _____ _____

B. MATCHING

1. Stand   your name.
2. Write   down.
3. Open   up.
4. Sit   your book.

C. WHAT'S THE ACTION?

Close	Give	Raise	Work
Erase	Go	Read	Write

1. ___Write___ your name.

2. _____ to the board.

3. _____ your book.

4. _____ the answer.

5. _____ your hand.

6. _____ your name.

7. _____ page eight.

8. _____ in groups.

A. LISTENING

Listen. Put a check under the correct picture.

1. _____   2. _____   _____

3. _____   _____   4. _____   _____

5. _____   _____   6. _____   _____

B. MATCHING

1. Watch   notes.

2. Do   the lights.

3. Turn off   your homework.

4. Take   the movie.

C. WHAT'S THE ACTION?

Answer	Correct	Lower	Turn off
Check	Do	Take	Watch

1. ___Check___ your answers.

2. _____ your mistakes.

3. _____ notes.

4. _____ the movie.

5. _____ the questions.

6. _____ your homework.

7. _____ the lights.

8. _____ the shades.

A. MATCHING

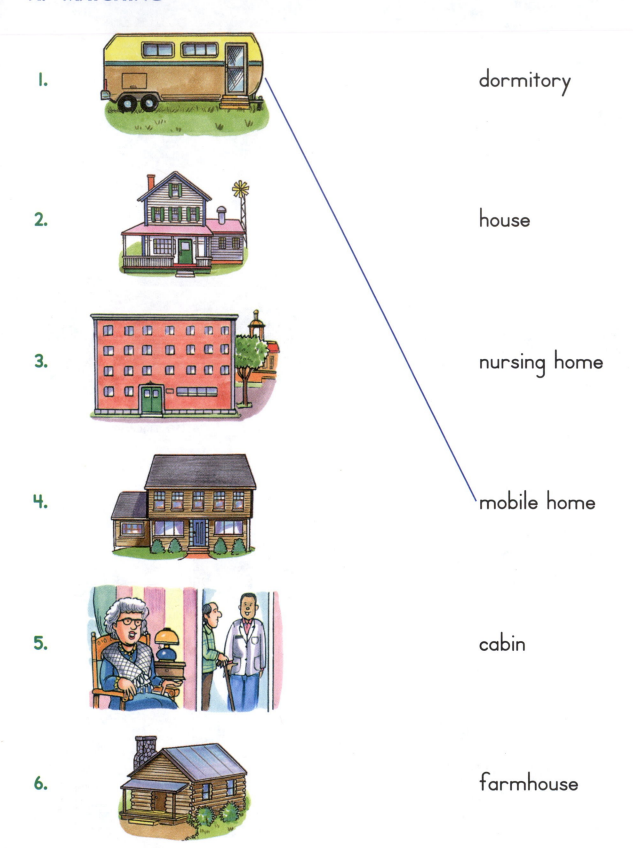

1.   dormitory

2.   house

3.   nursing home

4.   mobile home

5.   cabin

6.   farmhouse

B. CHOOSE THE CORRECT ANSWER

1. a. She lives in a house.
   (b.) She lives in an apartment.

2. a. He lives in a dormitory.
   b. He lives in a cabin.

3. a. They live in a trailer.
   b. They live in a houseboat.

4. a. She lives in a nursing home.
   b. She lives in a farmhouse.

C. WHAT TYPE OF HOUSING?

1. c a b i n

2. t _ _ _ _ _ _

3. h _ _ _ _

4. f _ _ _ _ _ _ _ _

5. a _ _ _ _ _ _ _ _

6. s _ _ _ _ _ _

THE LIVING ROOM

A. CIRCLE THE CORRECT WORD

1. sofa
   (armchair)

2. coffee table
   bookcase

3. rug
   pillow

4. lamp
   plant

5. floor
   wall

6. painting
   window

B. WHERE IS IT?

Look at page 20 of the dictionary. Write the correct word.

1. There's a <u>l a m p</u> on the end table.

2. There's a <u>p</u> _ _ _ _ _ _ on the bookcase.

3. There are <u>d</u> _ _ _ _ _ on the window.

4. There's a <u>p</u> _ _ _ _ _ _ _ on the wall.

5. There's a <u>p</u> _ _ _ _ _ on the sofa.

C. WHAT'S THE WORD?

| bookcase | lamp | plant | sofa | window |
| fireplace | pillow | rug | television | |

1. _____sofa_____   2. _____   3. _____

4. _____   5. _____   6. _____

7. _____   8. _____   9. _____

D. JOURNAL

In my living room there is _____

_____.

A. WHAT'S IN THE DINING ROOM?

1. <u>c a n d l e</u>

2. <u>t</u> _ _ _ _

3. <u>c</u> _ _ _ _

4. <u>p</u> _ _ _ _ _ _

5. <u>t</u> _ _ _ _ _

B. MATCHING

1. china   bowl

2. salt   dish

3. butter   shaker

4. salad   pot

5. coffee   cabinet

C. LISTENING

Listen and circle the words you hear.

1. (butter dish)   salt shaker   4. table   tablecloth

2. teapot   pitcher   5. teapot   coffee pot

3. salt shaker   pepper shaker   6. creamer   sugar bowl

22

A. CHOOSE THE CORRECT ANSWER

1. (a.) The cup goes on the saucer.
   b. The saucer goes on the cup.

2. a. The napkin goes on the fork.
   b. The fork goes on the napkin.

3. a. The knife goes to the right of the teaspoon.
   b. The teaspoon goes to the right of the knife.

4. a. The soup spoon goes to the right of the teaspoon.
   b. The soup spoon goes to the left of the teaspoon.

B. WHAT IS IT?

1. g l a s s   2. c _ _   3. n _ _ _ _ _

4. t _ _ _ _ _ _ _   5. k _ _ _ _   6. f _ _ _

A. WHAT'S THE WORD?

bed	blanket	blinds	dresser	mirror	pillow

1. _____pillow_____

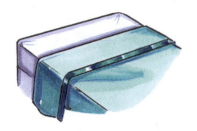

2. _____

3. _____

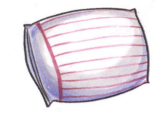

4. _____

5. _____

6. _____

B. MATCHING

1. night   radio

2. alarm   spring

3. jewelry   clock

4. twin   table

5. clock   box

6. box   bed

C. WHERE IS IT?

Look at page 26 of the dictionary. Write the correct word.

1. The alarm clock is on the <u>n i g h t s t a n d</u>.

2. The pillow is on the _ _ _.

3. The jewelry box is on the _ _ _ _ _ _ _ _.

4. The _ _ _ _ _ is between the bed and the bureau.

5. The _ _ _ _ _ _ is over the dresser.

6. The _ _ _ _ _ _ are on the window.

D. LISTENING

Listen and circle the words you hear.

1. (blanket)
   blinds

2. mattress
   dresser

3. bedspread
   box spring

4. dresses
   mirror

5. pillow
   blanket

6. alarm clock
   clock radio

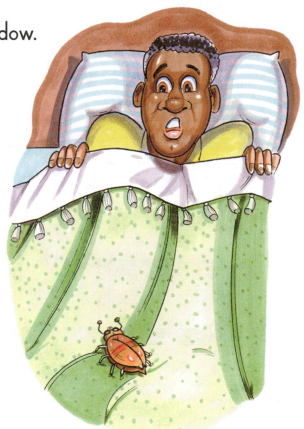

E. JOURNAL

In my bedroom there is _____

_____

_____.

A. WHAT'S IN THE KITCHEN?

cabinet	oven	sponge	dishwasher	refrigerator
stove	sink	toaster	microwave	

1. <u>dishwasher</u>

2. _____

3. _____

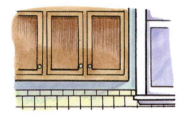

4. _____

5. _____

6. _____

7. _____

8. _____

9. _____

B. WHICH GROUP?

dishwasher	microwave	range	sink

For cooking:

_____ microwave _____

_____

For cleaning:

_____

_____

C. MATCHING

1. garbage   opener

2. can   board

3. dish   maker

4. cutting   rack

5. kitchen   pail

6. ice   chair

D. WORDSEARCH

```
C  T  B  O  P  N  X  C  A  B  I  N  E  T
O  D  A  V  R  W  S  M  Q  Z  G  A  B  O
U  B  S  E  C  P  T  B  C  M  P  L  V  A
N  S  I  N  K  L  O  U  W  M  E  K  C  S
T  J  I  S  T  R  V  T  O  P  Q  B  E  T
E  J  R  Q  Y  A  E  J  G  O  F  S  W  E
R  C  P  U  D  I  S  H  W  A  S  H  E  R
T  B  P  M  B  S  L  A  M  E  P  A  F  O
F  R  E  E  Z  E  R  E  P  O  C  V  F  Z
```

___ CABINET   ___ FREEZER   ___ STOVE

___ COUNTER   ✓ OVEN   ___ TOASTER

___ DISHWASHER   ✓ SINK

A. WHAT IS IT?

| car seat | doll | stroller | crib | high chair | swing |

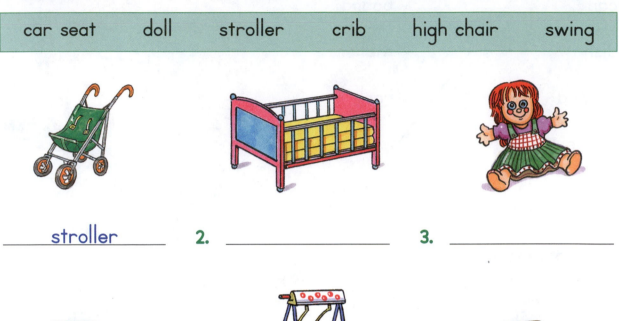

1. _____stroller_____ 2. _____ 3. _____

4. _____ 5. _____ 6. _____

B. MATCHING

Look at page 30 of the dictionary. Complete the sentences.

1. The doll is   in the crib.

2. The baby is   next to the changing table.

3. The intercom is   in the playpen.

4. The stuffed animal is   in the toy chest.

5. The diaper pail is   on the chest.

BABY CARE

A. WHAT IS IT?

1. <u>o i n t m e n t</u>

2. <u>b</u> _ _ _ _ _ _

3. <u>n</u> _ _ _ _ _ _

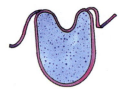

4. <u>b</u> _ _

5. <u>p</u> _ _ _ _ _ _ _

6. <u>b</u> _ _ _ _ _ _ _

B. MATCHING

1. baby   swabs

2. diaper   powder

3. teething   ring

4. cotton   diapers

5. disposable   pins

C. LISTENING

Listen. Write the number under the correct picture.

___   ___   <u>1</u>   ___   ___   ___

A. WHAT'S IN THE BATHROOM?

bath mat	mirror	shower	soap	toothbrush
bathtub	plunger	sink	toilet	

1. ___plunger___

2. _____

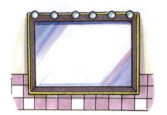

3. _____

4. _____

5. _____

6. _____

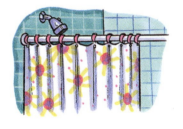

7. _____

8. _____

9. _____

B. LISTENING

Listen and circle the word you hear.

1. mat   (mirror)
2. sink   scale
3. towel   shower

4. toilet   towel
5. plunger   sponge
6. cup   tub

A. WHAT IS IT?

1. <u>c o m b</u>

2. r _ _ _ _ _

3. _ _ _ _ _ _ _ _ _ _

4. _ _ _ _ _ _ _

5. _ _ _ _ _ _ _ _

6. _ _ _ _ _ _ _ _ _

B. WHICH GROUP?

brush	conditioner	mouthwash	toothbrush
comb	dental floss	shampoo	toothpaste

For teeth

dental floss

_____

_____

_____

For hair

_____

_____

_____

_____

C. LISTENING

Listen. Write the correct number.

___ comb   ___ scissors   ___ shampoo

___ powder   _1_ hair brush   ___ toothpaste

A. WHAT IS IT?

1. b r o o m

2. m _ _

3. d _ _ _ _ _ _

4. _ _ _ _

5. _ _ _ _ _ _

6. _ _ _ _ _ _

B. MATCHING

Look at page 38 of the dictionary. Complete the sentences.

1. The washer is   in the bucket.

2. The broom is   next to the dryer.

3. The trash can is   on the clothesline.

4. The clothespins are   next to the dustpan.

5. The scrub brush is   next to the utility sink.

C. LISTENING

Listen and circle the words you hear.

1. (broom)   bucket   4. clothesline   clothespins

2. dryer   iron   5. bucket   pail

3. dustpan   trash can   6. sponge   scrub

A. WHAT IS IT?

chimney	lamppost	mailbox	garage	lawnmower	window

1. _____mailbox_____

2. _____

3. _____

4. _____

5. _____

6. _____

B. MATCHING

1. doorbell   garage

2. letter   lawnmower

3. television   door

4. grass   mailbox

5. car   TV antenna

A. CHOOSE THE CORRECT WORD

1. smoke detector
   (fire alarm)

2. buzzer
   peephole

3. intercom
   elevator

4. balcony
   lobby

5. garbage chute
   laundry room

6. parking lot
   parking garage

B. MATCHING

1. laundry   conditioner

2. swimming   lot

3. parking   room

4. smoke   chute

5. garbage   pool

6. air   detector

HOUSING UTILITIES, SERVICES, AND REPAIRS

A. WHO IS IT?

| carpenter   electrician   gardener   locksmith   painter   plumber |

1. __locksmith__

2. _____

3. _____

4. _____

5. _____

6. _____

B. MATCHING: WHO REPAIRS IT?

1. television   plumber

2. sink   locksmith

3. steps   electrician

4. light   carpenter

5. door lock   TV repair person

A. WHAT IS IT?

1. <u>s a w</u>

2. <u>h</u> _ _ _ _ _ _

3. <u>p</u> _ _ _ _ _

4. <u>w</u> _ _ _ _ _

5. <u>d</u> _ _ _ _

6. <u>s</u> _ _ _ _ _ _ _ _ _

7. <u>h</u> _ _ _

8. <u>r</u> _ _ _

9. <u>s</u> _ _ _ _ _

B. LISTENING

Listen. Write the correct number.

___ hammer

___ saw

___ shovel

___ sandpaper

<u>1</u> electric drill

___ lawnmower

CARDINAL NUMBERS

A. MATCHING

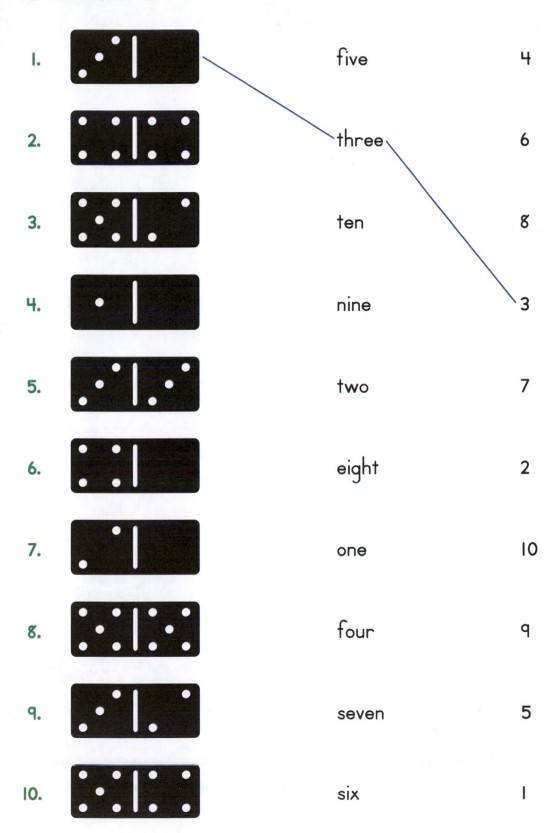

1.	five	4
2.	three	6
3.	ten	8
4.	nine	3
5.	two	7
6.	eight	2
7.	one	10
8.	four	9
9.	seven	5
10.	six	1

B. WHAT'S THE NUMBER?

1. seven   _7_
2. nine   _____
3. two   _____
4. ten   _____
5. eight   _____

6. fifty   _9_
7. thirty   _____
8. one hundred   _____
9. twenty-one   _____
10. sixty-two   _____

C. WHAT'S THE WORD?

3   _three_
1   _____
5   _____
4   _____
20   _____

15   _____
11   _____
12   _____
22   _____
36   _____

D. LISTENING

Listen and circle the number you hear.

1. (13)   30
2. 14   40
3. 19   90
4. 8   80

5. 17   70
6. 16   60
7. 42   24
8. 35   53

ORDINAL NUMBERS

A. MATCHING

1.	third	9th
2.	ninth	60th
3.	first	12th
4.	twelfth	3rd
5.	sixtieth	1st

6.	eleventh	80th
7.	eighth	11th
8.	fourth	14th
9.	eightieth	4th
10.	fourteenth	8th

B. WHAT'S THE NUMBER?

1. second _____2nd_____
2. tenth _____
3. thirteenth _____
4. first _____
5. fiftieth _____

C. WHAT'S THE WORD?

14th _____fourteenth_____
6th _____
60th _____
11th _____
20th _____

D. MATCHING

1.	four	fifth
2.	five	second
3.	two	fourth
4.	one	third
5.	three	tenth
6.	ten	first

E. LISTENING

Listen and circle the number you hear.

1.	4th	(14th)	40th
2.	7th	17th	70th
3.	3rd	13th	30th
4.	8th	18th	80th
5.	2nd	22nd	32nd

A. MATCHING

1.  3X2=6

2. 8 ÷ 2 = 4

3. $\frac{9}{-2}$ = 7

4. $\frac{+\frac{1}{4}}{5}$

subtraction

addition

multiplication

division

B. MATCHING

1. minus   ×

2. times   +

3. equals   −

4. plus   ÷

5. divided by   =

C. LISTENING

Listen and circle the answer.

1.   +   −   ⊗   ÷

2.   +   −   ×   ÷

3.   +   −   ×   ÷

4.   +   −   ×   ÷

5.   +   −   ×   ÷

D. WRITE THE MATH PROBLEMS

1. One plus three equals four.

$$\frac{1}{+3} = \frac{}{4}$$

2. Eight divided by four is two.

3. Two times five equals ten.

4. Twelve minus seven is five.

E. WHAT'S THE FRACTION?

<u>1/4</u> _____ _____ _____ _____

F. MATCHING

1. one half   2/3

2. one quarter   3/4

3. two thirds   1/2

4. three fourths   1/3

5. one third   1/4

G. LISTENING

Listen and circle the answer.

1. (1/3)   1/4

2. 1/4   1/2

3. 1/4   3/4

4. 1/4   3/4

5. 1/2   2/3

H. WHAT'S THE PERCENT?

<u>75%</u> _____ _____ _____

I. MATCHING

1. fifty percent   25%

2. twenty-five percent   50%

3. one hundred percent   30%

4. thirty percent   75%

5. seventy-five percent   100%

J. LISTENING

Listen and write the percent you hear.

1. <u>50%</u>   4. _____

2. _____   5. _____

3. _____   6. _____

A.   WHAT TIME IS IT?

8:00 _____ _____ _____

_____ _____ _____ _____

B.   CHOOSE THE CORRECT ANSWER

1. (a.) It's a quarter to four.
   b. It's a quarter to three.

2. a. It's seven thirty.
   b. It's six thirty.

3. a. It's five thirty.
   b. It's six twenty-five.

4. a. It's a quarter to five.
   b. It's a quarter after five.

C. MATCHING

1. a quarter to four   4:30   ten to five

2. four twenty   4:15   three forty-five

3. half past four   3:45   four thirty

4. a quarter after four   4:50   twenty after four

5. four fifty   4:20   four fifteen

D. CHOOSE THE CORRECT TIME

1. (7:00 A.M.)   2. noon   3. noon   4. 10:00 A.M.

    7:00 P.M.   midnight   midnight   10:00 P.M.

E. LISTENING

Listen and circle the time you hear.

1. 2:30   (8:30)   4. 5:45   6:45

2. 10:00   2:00   5. 1:30   2:30

3. 3:15   4:15   6. 5:01   1:05

F. JOURNAL: MY DAILY SCHEDULE

I get up at _____. I eat breakfast at _____.

I go to school at _____. I have lunch at _____.

I eat dinner at _____. I go to sleep at _____.

43

A. WHAT'S MISSING?

1. Ja_nuary
2. F_bruary
3. Ma_ch
4. A_ _il
5. M_ _
6. J_ _e

7. J_ _y
8. A_g_ _t
9. S_ _t_ _ber
10. O_ _o_er
11. N_ _ _ _ _ _ _
12. D_ _ _ _ _ _ _

B. WRITE THE MONTH

1. January __February__ March
2. March April _____
3. June _____ August
4. August _____ October
5. October November _____

C. WHAT'S MISSING?

1. Su_nday
2. Mo_day
3. Tue_d_ _
4. We_nes_ _ _

5. Th_ _ _day
6. F_ _ _ _ _
7. S_ _ _ _ _ _ _

D. WRITE THE DAY

1. Sun.   ___Sunday___
2. Mon.   _____
3. Tue.   _____
4. Wed.   _____
5. Thur.   _____
6. Fri.   _____
7. Sat.   _____

E. MATCHING

1. 7/10/98   March 6, 1997
2. 5/8/99   January 2, 1999
3. 1/2/99   February 1, 1999
4. 2/1/99   July 10, 1998
5. 3/6/97   May 8, 1999

F. WRITING

1. What day is it?   It's _____.
2. What year is it?   It's _____.
3. What month is it?   It's _____.
4. What's today's date?   Today is _____.

G. LISTENING

Listen and circle the correct answer.

1. (Monday)   Sunday
2. Thursday   Tuesday
3. June   July
4. November   December
5. April 4   April 14
6. May 7   March 7

45

A. WHAT'S THE PLACE?

bank	bakery	bus station
clinic	book store	coffee shop

1. ___clinic___

2. _____

3. _____

4. _____

5. _____

6. _____

B. MATCHING

1. cake   bank

2. money   cafeteria

3. hair   cleaners

4. food   barber shop

5. suit   bakery

PLACES AROUND TOWN II

A. WHAT'S THE PLACE?

hospital	hair salon	grocery store
drug store	gas station	hardware store

1. __grocery store__

2. _____

3. _____

4. _____

5. _____

6. _____

B. MATCHING

1.   tools   florist

2.   medicine   grocery store

3.   bread   gas station

4.   car   hardware store

5.   flowers   drug store

A. WHAT'S THE PLACE?

| park | library | pet shop |
| museum | laundromat | parking lot |

1. _____museum_____

2. _____

3. _____

4. _____

5. _____

6. _____

B. WORDSEARCH

```
I  L A U N D R O M A T  N A M
U Z D G O A J M O J N B E U
S U N R P T M D T D S N V S
L I B R A R Y R E T I N E E
U J L U R O G U L D U N H U
V R U T K D R M J U Z G Z M
```

___ PARK   ___ LIBRARY   ✔ LAUNDROMAT

___ MOTEL   ___ MUSEUM

48

A. WHAT'S THE PLACE?

zoo	restaurant	supermarket
school	post office	shopping mall

1. _____school_____

2. _____

3. _____

4. _____

5. _____

6. _____

B. MATCHING

1. eggs   train station

2. letter   supermarket

3.  teacher   school

4.  dinner   post office

5.  train   restaurant

A. WHAT'S THE WORD?

bus	bus stop	street	taxi driver
taxi	sidewalk	parking meter	meter maid

1. _____meter maid_____

3. _____

2. _____

4. _____

5. _____

7. _____

6. _____

8. _____

B. YES OR NO?

Look at page 64 of the dictionary. Answer <u>Yes</u> or <u>No</u>.

<u>No</u> 1. The taxi is on the sidewalk.

_____ 2. The trash container is on the sidewalk.

_____ 3. The police station is next to the courthouse.

_____ 4. The bus is in front of a taxi.

_____ 5. The bus stop is in front of the police station.

A. WHAT'S THE WORD?

crosswalk	intersection	pedestrian
street sign	traffic light	police officer

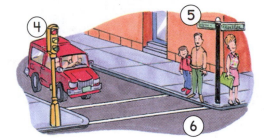

1. _____pedestrian_____

2. _____

3. _____

4. _____

5. _____

6. _____

B. MATCHING

1. traffic   stand

2. phone   officer

3. taxi   light

4. police   truck

5. garbage   booth

C. WHICH GROUP?

intersection	**People**	**Places**
pedestrian	_____pedestrian_____	_____
police officer		
fire station	_____	_____
street vendor		
taxi stand	_____	_____

DESCRIBING PEOPLE AND THINGS 1

A. WHAT'S THE WORD?

cold	hot	loose	new	short	tall
high	large	low	old	small	tight

1. _____ new _____
2. _____

3. _____
4. _____

5. _____
6. _____

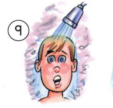

7. _____
8. _____

9. _____
10. _____

11. _____
12. _____

B. MATCHING: OPPOSITES

1. fast   low
2. big   light
3. heavy   tight
4. high   little
5. loose   slow

6. wide   light
7. old   narrow
8. good   cold
9. dark   bad
10. hot   young

C. WHAT'S THE WORD?

| cold | curly | heavy | narrow | new | short | small | young |

1. Is his hair long?

   No. It's <u>s h o r t</u>.

2. Is the house large?

   No. It's _ _ _ _ _.

3. Is the street wide?

   No. It's _ _ _ _ _ _.

4. Is the water hot?

   No. It's _ _ _ _.

5. Is her hair straight?

   No. It's _ _ _ _ _.

6. Is the box light?

   No. It's _ _ _ _ _.

7. Is your car old?

   No. It's _ _ _.

8. Is your teacher old?

   No. She's _ _ _ _ _.

A. WHAT'S THE WORD?

clean	dirty	empty	full	neat	plain
closed	dry	fancy	messy	open	wet

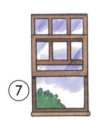

1. _____dry_____

2. _____

3. _____

4. _____

5. _____

6. _____

7. _____

8. _____

9. _____

10. _____

11. _____

12. _____

B. MATCHING: OPPOSITES

1. clean   plain

2. easy   married

3. fancy   dirty

4. single   cheap

5. expensive   difficult

6. soft   poor

7. handsome   hard

8. rich   rough

9. shiny   dull

10. smooth   ugly

C. WHAT'S THE WORD?

closed	dry	dull	easy	neat	plain	single	soft

1. Is the homework difficult?

   No. It's <u>e a s y</u>.

2. Is she married?

   No. She's _ _ _ _ _ _ _.

3. Is the bank open?

   No. It's _ _ _ _ _ _.

4. Are the clothes wet?

   No. They're _ _ _.

5. Is the dress fancy?

   No. It's _ _ _ _ _.

6. Is your room messy?

   No. It's _ _ _ _.

7. Is the knife sharp?

   No. It's _ _ _ _.

8. Is the mattress hard?

   No. It's _ _ _ _.

A. LISTENING

Listen. Put a check under the correct picture.

1. _____   ✓   2. _____   _____

3. _____   _____   4. _____   _____

5. _____   _____   6. _____   _____

B. WHAT'S THE WORD?

1. s a d   2. _ _ _ _ _   3. _ _ _ _ _ _ _ _

4. _ _ _ _ _   5. _ _ _ _ _   6. _ _ _ _ _ _

A. CHOOSE THE CORRECT WORD

1. confused
   (proud)

2. disgusted
   scared

3. worried
   surprised

4. mad
   embarrassed

5. angry
   nervous

6. jealous
   afraid

B. LISTENING

Listen. Write the number under the correct picture.

_____   _____   _____   1   _____   _____

C. JOURNAL

I feel _____ today
(happy / sad / tired / angry / worried / proud)

because _____

_____.

57

A. WHAT'S THE WORD?

apple	grapes	lime	peach	plum
banana	lemon	orange	pear	

1. _____lemon_____

2. _____

3. _____

4. _____

5. _____

6. _____

7. _____

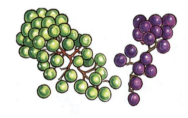

8. _____

9. _____

B. LISTENING

Listen and circle the fruit you hear.

1. (cherries)   cranberries   4. banana   papaya

2. limes   lemons   5. grapes   dates

3. plums   prunes   6. tangerine   nectarine

A. WHAT'S THE WORD?

1. o n i o n

2. t _ _ _ _ _

3. c _ _ _ _ _

4. _ _ _ _ _ _ _

5. _ _ _ _ _ _

6. _ _ _ _ _ _ _ _

7. _ _ _ _

8. _ _ _ _ _ _

9. _ _ _ _ _ _ _

B. MATCHING

1. acorn   potato

2. red   bean

3. sweet   squash

4. lima   sprout

5. brussels   pepper

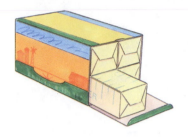
A. WHAT'S THE WORD?

1.  m i l k

2. _ _ _ _ _ _ _

3. _ _ _ _ _ _ _

4. _ _ _ _ _ _

5. _ _ _ _

6. _ _ _ _ _ _

7. _ _ _ _ _ _ _   _ _ _ _ _

8. _ _ _ _ _ _   _ _ _ _ _

9. _ _ _ _   _ _ _ _ _

10. _ _ _ _ _ _ _   _ _ _ _ _

A. WHAT'S THE WORD?

bread	cookies	juice	mayonnaise	salt	soup
cereal	flour	ketchup	rice	soda	spaghetti

1. _____ketchup_____

2. _____

3. _____

4. _____

5. _____

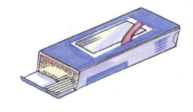

6. _____

7. _____

8. _____

9. _____

10. _____

11. _____

12. _____

B. MATCHING

1. toilet   sauce

2. soy   towels

3. salad   paper

4. ice   dressing

5. paper   cream

C. WHAT'S THE WORD?

1. <u>r o l l s</u>

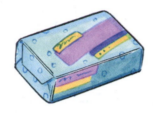

2. _ _ _ _

3. _ _ _ _ _ _ _ _

4. _ _ _ _ _ _ _ _

5. _ _ _ _

6. _ _ _ _ _ _ _ _

7. _ _ _ _ _

8. _ _ _

9. _ _ _ _ _ _ _

A. CHOOSE THE CORRECT WORD

1. (lamb)
   ham

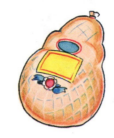

2. bacon
   turkey

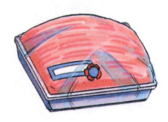

3. ground beef
   fish

4. clams
   crabs

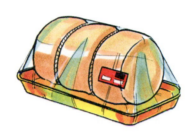

5. chicken
   pork

6. shrimp
   lobster

B. WHAT'S THE WORD?

1. f i s h

2. c _ _ _ _ _ _ _

3. s _ _ _ _ _

4. _ _ _

5. _ _ _ _ _ _

6. _ _ _ _ _ _ _

A. CHOOSE THE CORRECT WORD

1. customer
   (cashier)

2. aisle
   scale

3. shopper
   packer

4. scale
   cash register

5. plastic bag
   paper bag

6. scale
   counter

7. shopping cart
   checkout counter

8. plastic bag
   shopping basket

B. WHICH GROUP?

bagger	paper bag
cashier	scale
counter	shopper

People

bagger

Things

A. WHAT'S THE WORD?

bag	bar	box	bunch	can	dozen

1. a __dozen__ eggs

4. a _____ of carrots

2. a _____ of soup

5. a _____ of crackers

3. a _____ of flour

6. a _____ of soap

B. MATCHING

1. a bar of   soup

2. a box of   eggs

3. a bottle of   ketchup

4. a bunch of   cereal

5. a can of   soap

6. a dozen   cottage cheese

7. a container of   bananas

A. WHAT'S THE WORD?

gallon	liter	loaf	pint	pound	quart

 1. a ___pint___ of ice cream

 4. a _____ of butter

 2. a _____ of milk

 5. a _____ of soda

 3. a _____ of bread

 6. a _____ of milk

B. MATCHING

1. a jar of   orange juice

2. a loaf of   apples

3. a package of   rolls

4. a pound of   mustard

5. a half-gallon of   bread

6. a pint of   paper towels

7. a roll of   sour cream

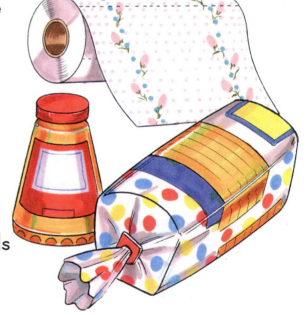

FOOD PREPARATION AND RECIPES

A. CHOOSE THE CORRECT WORD

1. stir
   (slice)

2. bake
   boil

3. mix
   grate

4. fry
   steam

5. peel
   pour

6. beat
   cut

B. MATCHING

1.    Chop   the potatoes.

2.    Bake   the eggs.

3.    Peel   the onions.

4.    Scramble   the vegetables.

5.    Stir-fry   the orange.

A. WHAT'S THE WORD?

1. m u f f i n

2. b _ _ _ _ _

3. l _ _ _ _ _ _ _ _

4. _ _ _ _ _ _

5. _ _ _ _ _

6. _ _ _ _ _ _ _ _

7. _ _ _   _ _ _

8. _ _ _

9. _ _ _ _

B. WHICH GROUP?

| coffee | donut | hot dog | hamburger | lemonade | milk | taco | tea |

eat   drink

____taco____   _____ | _____   _____

_____   _____ | _____   _____

C. LISTENING

Listen. Write the number under the correct picture.

____   ____ 1   ____

A. WHAT'S THE WORD?

booth	cook	high chair	table	waitress
cashier	dishwasher	menu	waiter	

1. ___booth___

2. _____

3. _____

4. _____

5. _____

6. _____

7. _____

8. _____

9. _____

B. LISTENING

Listen. Write the number under the correct picture.

___   ___   ___   _1_   ___   ___

COLORS

A. WHAT'S THE COLOR?

 1. <u>r e d</u>

 2. <u>b</u> _ _ _

 3. <u>b</u> _ _ _ _

 4. _ _ _ _ _

 5. _ _ _ _ _ _

 6. _ _ _ _

 7. _ _ _ _ _ _

 8. _ _ _ _ _

 9. _ _ _ _ _

B. CROSSWORD

ACROSS

2.   4.

DOWN

1.   2.   3.

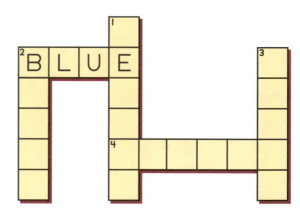

C. JOURNAL

My hair is _____.

My eyes are _____.

My favorite color is _____.

A. WHAT'S THE WORD?

blouse	jacket	shirt	skirt	sweater
dress	pants	shorts	suit	

1. _____shirt_____

2. _____

3. _____

4. _____

5. _____

6. _____

7. _____

8. _____

9. _____

B. LISTENING

Listen and circle the word you hear.

1. dress   (blouse)   4. tie   vest

2. jacket   slacks   5. suit   shorts

3. skirt   shirt   6. skirt   shirt

SLEEPWEAR, UNDERWEAR, AND FOOTWEAR

A. WHAT'S THE WORD?

1. <u>s t o c k i n g s</u>

2. p _ _ _ _ _ _ _

3. s _ _ _ _ _

4. _ _ _ _ _

5. _ _ _ _ _ _ _ _

6. _ _ _ _ _

7. _ _ _ _ _ _ _ _ _

8. _ _ _ _ _ _ _

9. _ _ _ _ _ _ _ _

B. WHICH GROUP?

| boots | briefs | nightgown | pajamas | shoes | undershirt |

Sleepwear	Underwear	Footwear
nightgown	_____	_____
_____	_____	_____

72

A. WHAT'S THE WORD?

| hat | gloves | poncho | rubbers | swimsuit |
| coat | jacket | mittens | raincoat | |

1. _____rubbers_____

2. _____

3. _____

4. _____

5. _____

6. _____

7. _____

8. _____

9. _____

B. WHICH GROUP?

| coat | gloves | poncho | raincoat | rubbers | scarf |

It's raining!   It's cold!

_____poncho_____   _____

_____   _____

_____   _____

JEWELRY AND ACCESSORIES

A. CHOOSE THE CORRECT WORD

1. (earrings)
   cuff links

2. belt
   necklace

3. umbrella
   briefcase

4. wallet
   watch

5. backpack
   purse

6. ring
   key ring

B. MATCHING

1. wedding	bag
2. change	band
3. book	ring
4. cuff	links
5. key	purse

A. WHAT'S THE WORD?

fancy	high	large	loose	plain	small
heavy	light	long	low	short	tight

1. _____tight_____   3. _____   5. _____

2. _____   4. _____   6. _____

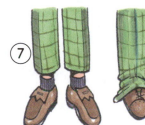

7. _____   9. _____   11. _____

8. _____   10. _____   12. _____

B. MATCHING: OPPOSITES

1. long   baggy

2. dark   plain

3. tight   short

4. fancy   narrow

5. wide   light

COINS

A. WHAT IS IT?

1. <u>n i c k e l</u>

    <u>5¢</u>   <u>$.05</u>

2. _ _ _ _ _ _

    _____ _____

3. _ _ _ _ _ _ _ _

    _____ _____

4. _ _ _ _ _ _ _ _ _ _

    _____ _____

5. _ _ _ _

    _____ _____

B. WHAT'S THE AMOUNT?

| $.05 | $.12 | $.15 | $.25 | $.26 | $.30 | $.75 | $1.00 |

1.   <u>$.05</u>

2. _____

3. _____

4. _____

5. _____

6. _____

7. _____

8. _____

A. MATCHING

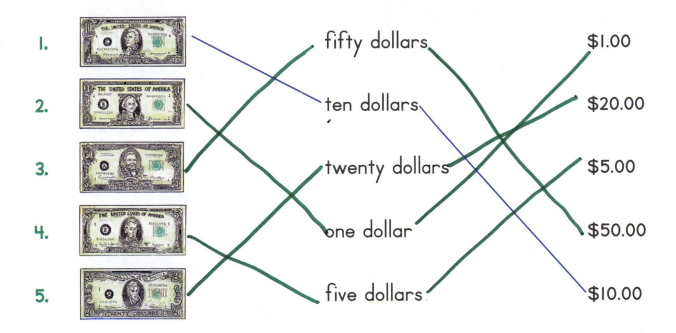

1.
2.
3.
4.
5.

fifty dollars $1.00

ten dollars $20.00

twenty dollars $5.00

one dollar $50.00

five dollars $10.00

B. WHAT'S THE AMOUNT?

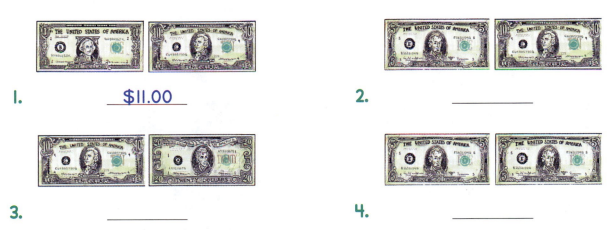

1. $11.00

2. _____

3. _____

4. _____

C. LISTENING

Listen and circle the amount you hear.

1. ($35.00) $.35   4. $16.00 $61.00

2. $.05 $5.00   5. $7.10 $71.00

3. $.44 $44.00   6. $14.41 $41.14

A. CHOOSE THE CORRECT WORD

1. bank book
   (check)

2. credit card
   checkbook

3. withdrawal slip
   money order

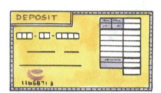

4. deposit slip
   ATM card

5. checkbook
   bank book

6. teller
   security guard

B. WRITE A CHECK

Write a check to a store.

Date __December 12, 2001__

Pay to the
order of __Acme Discount Store__ $ __30.15__

__Thirty and 15/100__   Dollars

Memo _____   _Ana Lopez_

1:2110783

Date _____

Pay to the
order of _____ $ _____

_____   Dollars

Memo _____   _____

1:2110783

C. AT THE BANK

Your account number is 3758 9402.

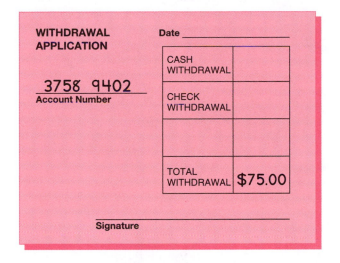

1. Withdraw $75.00.

2. Withdraw $200.00.

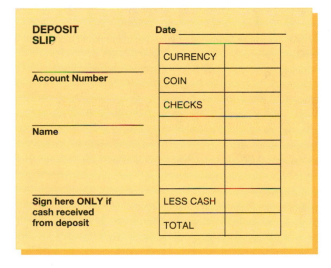

3. Deposit $300.00.

4. Deposit $195.00.

A. WHAT IS IT?

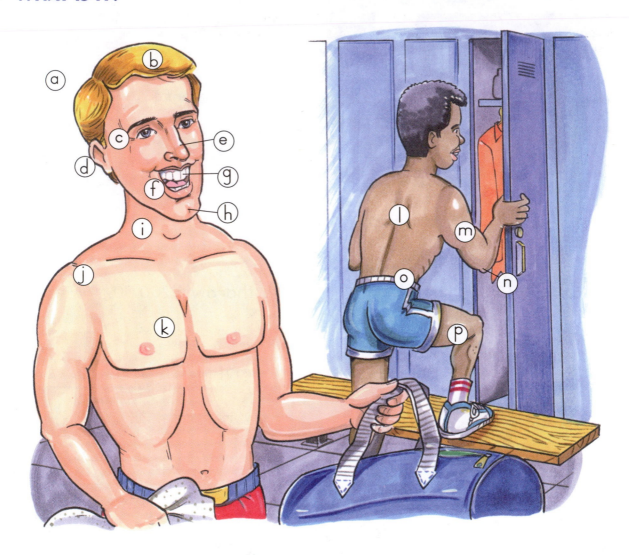

a. <u>h e a d</u>

b. _ _ _ _

c. _ _ _

d. _ _ _

e. _ _ _ _

f. _ _ _ _ _

g. _ _ _ _

h. _ _ _ _

i. _ _ _ _

j. _ _ _ _ _ _ _

k. _ _ _ _ _

l. _ _ _ _

m. _ _ _

n. _ _ _ _

o. _ _ _ _ _

p. _ _ _

A. WHAT IS IT?

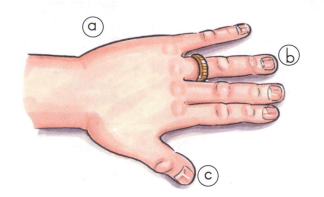

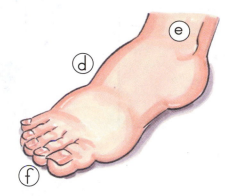

a. <u>h a n d</u>

b. _ _ _ _ _ _

c. _ _ _ _ _

d. _ _ _ _

e. _ _ _ _ _

f. _ _ _

B. MATCHING: WHERE ARE THEY?

1. toenail   foot

2. finger   toe

3. heel   neck

4. brain   hand

5. throat   head

C. HOW MANY DO WE HAVE?

1. feet   2

2. toes   _____

3. stomachs   _____

4. lungs   _____

5. fingers   _____

6. hearts   _____

7. thumbs   _____

8. livers   _____

A. CHOOSE THE CORRECT WORD

1. rash
   (insect bite)

2. headache
   earache

3. stomachache
   backache

4. sunburn
   fever

5. cough
   cavity

6. wart
   toothache

7. cold
   rash

8. sore throat
   stiff neck

9. the chills
   the hiccups

B. LISTENING

Listen and circle the word you hear.

1. earache   (headache)   4. rash   virus

2. cold   cough   5. fever   cavity

3. stomachache   backache   6. chills   hiccups

AILMENTS, SYMPTOMS, AND INJURIES II

A. CHOOSE THE CORRECT WORD

1. congested
   (dizzy)

2. burn
   bruise

3. cut
   twist

4. congested
   exhausted

5. cough
   sprain

6. scratch
   sneeze

B. WORDSEARCH

```
V  F  D  H  R  B  M  P  C  D  I  E  G  H
Q  D  I  V  E  R  M  D  O  O  R  M  S  F
C  Q  Z  I  S  L  F  B  U  R  N  N  N  E
U  L  Z  U  V  H  E  B  G  A  D  H  E  V
A  U  Y  R  A  C  T  L  H  Q  H  U  E  E
T  S  C  R  A  P  E  E  P  A  S  D  Z  W
P  S  V  N  B  X  R  N  T  W  J  U  E  Q
Z  F  N  O  P  W  R  T  W  I  S  T  H  B
```

✓ BURN   ___ DIZZY   ___ SNEEZE

✓ COUGH   ___ SCRAPE   ___ TWIST

A. CHOOSE THE CORRECT WORD

1. doctor
   (dentist)

2. pediatrician
   hygienist

3. lab technician
   X-ray technician

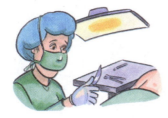

4. surgeon
   psychiatrist

5. cardiologist
   optometrist

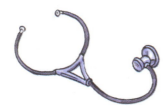

6. EMT
   nurse

7. drill
   stethoscope

8. thermometer
   needle

9. scale
   X-ray machine

B. MATCHING

1. blood
2. teeth
3. eyes
4. heart
5. children

dentist

optometrist

pediatrician

lab technician

cardiologist

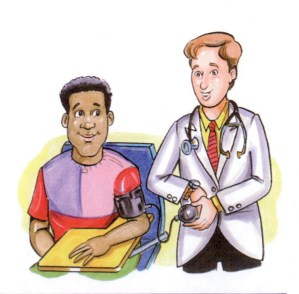

A. CHOOSE THE CORRECT WORD

1. (sling)
   bandaid

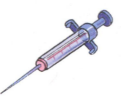

2. prescription
   injection

3. cast
   diet

4. gargle
   exercise

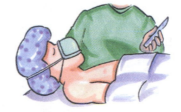

5. surgery
   counseling

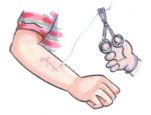

6. crutches
   stitches

7. I.V.
   X-ray

8. bed table
   hospital bed

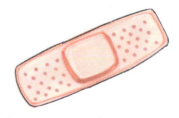

9. medical chart
   bandaid

B. MATCHING

1. physical   tests

2. blood   therapy

3. call   pan

4. bed   gown

5. hospital   button

A. CHOOSE THE CORRECT WORD

1. nasal spray
   (eye drops)

2. aspirin
   cough drops

3. throat lozenges
   antacid tablets

4. cough syrup
   vitamins

5. heating pad
   ice pack

6. ointment
   cold tablets

7. tablet
   capsule

8. pill
   caplet

9. teaspoon
   tablespoon

B. MATCHING

1. cough   spray

2. throat   pad

3. nasal   lozenges

4. heating   tablets

5. antacid   syrup

A. WHAT'S THE WORD?

stamp	mailbox	postcard	aerogramme	letter
zip code	package	envelope	money order	

1. _____envelope_____   2. _____   3. _____

4. _____   5. _____   6. _____

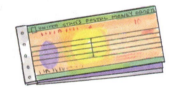

7. _____   8. _____   9. _____

B. MATCHING

1. letter   address

2. return   order

3. air   carrier

4. money   post

5. parcel   code

6. zip   mail

A. WHAT'S THE WORD?

atlas	magazine	librarian	card catalog
shelves	newspaper	encyclopedia	checkout desk

1. _____librarian_____

3. _____

2. _____

4. _____

5. _____

7. _____

6. _____

8. _____

B. LISTENING

Listen and circle the words you hear.

1. (card catalog)
   call card

2. newspapers
   magazines

3. library assistant
   librarian

4. dictionaries
   encyclopedias

5. atlases
   shelves

6. checkout desk
   information desk

A. WHERE ARE THEY?

1. The <u>p r i n c i p a l</u> is in
the _ _ _ _ _ _.

2. The _ _ _ _ _ _ is in the _ _ _.

3. The _ _ _ _ _ _ _ _ _ _ is in
the _ _ _ _ _ _ _ _ _.

4. The _ _ _ _ _ _ _ _ is in the
_ _ _ _ _ _ _ _ _ _ _ _ _ _.

5. The _ _ _ _ _ _ _ _ _
_ _ _ _ _ _ _ _ _ _ is in the
_ _ _ _ _ _ _ _ _ _ _ _ _ _ _.

6. The _ _ _ _ _ _ _ _ _ _ _ _
is in the _ _ _ _ _ ' _
_ _ _ _ _ _.

B. DRAW A DIAGRAM

Draw a picture of your school. Show the different rooms and
label them.

A. WHAT'S THE WORD?

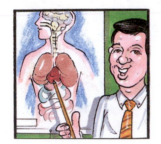

1. h e a l t h

2. h _ _ _ _ _ _

3. S _ _ _ _ _ _

4. E _ _ _ _ _ _ _

5. s _ _ _ _ _ _ _

6. m _ _ _

7. _ _ _

8. _ _ _ _ _

9. _ _ _ _ _ _ _ _ _

10. _ _ _ _ _ _ _ ' _ _

11. _ _ _ _ _   _ _ _ _ _ _ _ _

EXTRACURRICULAR ACTIVITIES

A. WHAT'S THE WORD?

band	football	school newspaper
choir	orchestra	literary magazine
drama	yearbook	student government

1. ____choir____

2. _____

3. _____

4. _____

5. _____

6. _____

7. _____

8. _____

9. _____

A. WHAT'S THE OCCUPATION?

1. <u>b u t c h e r</u>

2. _ _ _ _ _ _ _ _ _ _

3. _ _ _ _ _ _ _ _ _

4. _ _ _ _ _ _

5. _ _ _ _ _ _ _ _

6. _ _ _ _ _ _ _ _ _ _

B. MATCHING: WHO USES IT?

1.  calculator   carpenter

2. hammer   artist

3. paintbrush   accountant

4. cash register   barber

5. scissors   cashier

OCCUPATIONS II

A. WHAT'S THE OCCUPATION?

1. <u>g a r d e n e r</u>   2. _ _ _ _ _ _ _ _ _   3. _ _ _ _ _ _ _ _ _ _ _

4. _ _ _ _ _ _   5. _ _ _ _   6. _ _ _ _ _ _ _ _ _ _

B. MATCHING: WHO USES IT?

 1. broom — hairdresser

 2. saucepan — chef

 3. saw — gardener

 4. rake — custodian

 5. comb — construction worker

A. WHAT'S THE OCCUPATION?

1. p h a r m a c i s t

2. _ _ _ _ _ _ _ _

3. _ _ _ _ _ _ _ _ _ _ _

4. _ _ _ _ _ _ _ _ _

5. _ _ _ _ _ _ _ _

6. _ _ _ _ _ _

B. WORDSEARCH

```
L H F J T P O R E F P G I J
A F K X G L O F Q S A O U H
W T C L V U I Z O S I Q R H
Y O C X Y M E C H A N I C Z
E Z B U D B Y H P U T X G H
R H T Y D E V O S D E G C Z
S R E P O R T E R J R F H T
```

___ LAWYER ✓ PAINTER ___ REPORTER

___ MECHANIC ___ PLUMBER

A. WHAT'S THE OCCUPATION?

1. <u>s e c r e t a r y</u>

2. _ _ _ _ _ _ _

3. _ _ _ _ _ _ _ _ _ _

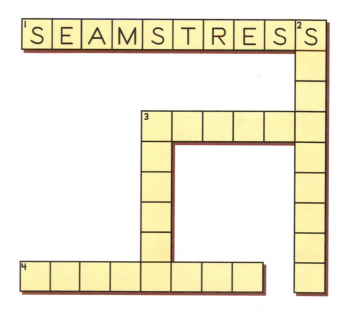

4. _ _ _ _ _ _ _

5. _ _ _ _ _ _ _ _

6. _ _ _ _ _ _   _ _ _ _

B. CROSSWORD

ACROSS

1.

3.

4.

DOWN

2.

3.

S E A M S T R E S S

WORK ACTIVITIES 1

A. WHAT DO THEY DO?

1. <u>c o o k</u>

2. _ _ _ _ _

3. _ _ _ _ _ _ _ _

4. _ _ _ _ _

5. _ _ _ _

6. _ _ _ _ _ _ _ _

B. MATCHING

1. Chefs   mow lawns.

2. Actors   build things.

3. Drivers   cook.

4. Gardeners   assemble components.

5. Assemblers   clean.

6. Carpenters   act.

7. Housekeepers   drive.

A. WHAT DO THEY DO?

1. p a i n t

2. _ _ _ _ _ _

3. _ _ _ _ _

4. _ _ _ _

5. _ _ _ _

6. _ _ _ _ _ _ _

B. MATCHING

1. A painter   types.

2. A secretary   sews.

3. A waiter   sells things.

4. A seamstress   serves food.

5. A salesperson   paints.

C. JOURNAL: MY WORK SKILLS

I can _____

_____ .

A. CHOOSE THE CORRECT WORD

1. (time clock)
   work station

2. suggestion box
   first-aid kit

3. cafeteria
   supply room

4. lever
   forklift

5. conveyor belt
   freight elevator

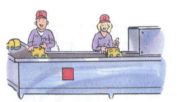

6. assembly line
   warehouse

7. safety glasses
   masks

8. loading dock
   hand truck

9. suggestion box
   lever

B. MATCHING

1. time   line
2. assembly   station
3. work   clock
4. first-aid   belt
5. conveyor   kit

A. WHAT'S THE WORD?

1. h e l m e t

2. _ _ _ _ _ _

3. _ _ _ _ _ _ _ _ _

4. _ _ _ _ _ _

5. _ _ _ _

6. _ _ _ _ _ _ _

7. _ _ _ _ _

8. _ _ _ _ _ _

9. _ _ _ _ _ _ _ _ _ _ _

B. WHICH GROUP?

beam	pipe	bulldozer
backhoe	plywood	cement mixer

Materials   Machines

beam

A. WHAT'S THE WORD?

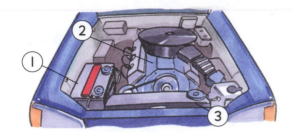

1. <u>b a t t e r y</u>

2. _ _ _ _ _ _

3. _ _ _ _ _ _ _ _

4. _ _ _ _

5. _ _ _ _ _ _ _ _ _

6. _ _ _ _ _ _ _

7. _ _ _   _ _ _ _ _ _ _

8. _ _ _   _ _ _ _

9. _ _ _ _ _ _ _ _

10. _ _ _ _ _

11. _ _ _ _ _

12. _ _ _ _ _   _ _ _ _

B. MATCHING

1. windshield   plate

2. rear   belt

3. license   defroster

4. spark   wipers

5. fan   plugs

A. CHOOSE THE CORRECT WORD

1. brake
   (seat belt)

2. steering column
   clutch

3. ignition
   accelerator

4. gearshift
   turn signal

5. speedometer
   ignition

6. visor
   rearview mirror

7. radio
   horn

8. dashboard
   air bag

9. turn signal
   stickshift

B. MATCHING

1. air — mirror
2. seat — bag
3. rearview — signal
4. turn — brake
5. emergency — belt

A. WHAT'S THE WORD?

taxi	subway	bus stop	bus driver	bus
train	luggage	conductor	bus station	

1. _____bus_____   2. _____   3. _____

4. _____   5. _____   6. _____

7. _____   8. _____   9. _____

B. MATCHING

1. passenger   counter

2. cab   driver

3. ticket   station

4. fare   car

5. subway   card

A. CHOOSE THE CORRECT WORD

1. (suitcase)
   garment bag

2. gate
   ticket

3. ticket agent
   customs officer

4. passport
   customs

5. security guard
   immigration officer

6. visa
   boarding pass

7. waiting area
   baggage claim area

8. metal detector
   arrival and departure monitor

B. MATCHING

1. immigration   counter

2. security   pass

3. ticket   guard

4. boarding   detector

5. metal   officer

A. WHAT'S THE WEATHER?

1. <u>c l e a r</u>

2. _ _ _ _ _ _ _ _

3. _ _ _ _ _

4. _ _ _ _ _

5. _ _ _ _ _

6. _ _ _ _ _ _

7. _ _ _ _ _ _

8. _ _ _ _ _

9. _ _ _ _ _ _ _ _ _

B. WHAT'S THE SEASON?

fall   spring   summer   winter

1. <u>winter</u>

2. _ _ _ _ _ _ _ _ _

3. _ _ _ _ _ _ _ _ _

4. _ _ _ _ _ _ _ _ _

C. CROSSWORD

ACROSS

3. 

5. 

6. 

7. 

DOWN

1. 

2. 

4. 

D. JOURNAL

My favorite season is ____________________

because ____________________

____

____________________.

A. WHAT'S THE WORD?

baseball	fishing	sailing	soccer
basketball	football	skating	swimming
bicycling	jogging	skiing	tennis

1. _____skating_____

2. _____

3. _____

4. _____

5. _____

6. _____

7. _____

8. _____

9. _____

10. _____

11. _____

12. _____

B. CROSSWORD

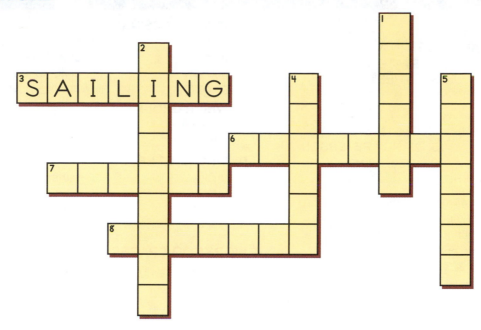

³S	A	I	L	I	N	G		

ACROSS

3.

6.

7.

8.

DOWN

1.

2.

4.

5.

C. JOURNAL

In my free time I like to _____

_____

_____

_____ .

WORKBOOK PAGES 1–3

A. CIRCLE THE SAME WORD
1. NAME
2. CITY
3. ADDRESS
4. STATE
5. STREET

B. MATCHING
1. CA
2. 22960
3. MAIN STREET
4. 684-1196
5. NANCY PETERSON
6. 045-61-8947

F. LISTENING
Listen and circle the words you hear.
1. A. What's your name?
   B. My name? John.
2. A. What's your zip code?
   B. My zip code? 22315.
3. A. What's your social security number?
   B. My social security number? 976-24-3069.
4. A. What's your street?
   B. My street? North Tenth Street.
5. A. What's your city?
   B. My city? Sacramento.
6. A. What's your first name?
   B. My first name? Ana.

Answers
1. name
2. zip code
3. social security
4. street
5. city
6. first

WORKBOOK PAGES 4–5

A. WHO ARE THEY?
1. b
2. f
3. d
4. e
5. c
6. a

B. MATCHING
1. father
2. sister
3. brother
4. mother
5. son
6. daughter

C. WHAT'S MISSING?
1. wife
   sister
2. father
   mother
3. husband
   son
4. grandson
   brother
5. baby
   daughter
6. grandmother
   grandfather

D. WHICH GROUP?
Parents:
1. father
2. mother
3. husband
4. wife

Children:
5. son
6. daughter
7. brother
8. sister

WORKBOOK PAGES 6–7

A. WHO ARE THEY?
1. d
2. a
3. c
4. e
5. b

B. WHAT'S MISSING?
1. aunt
   uncle
2. nephew
   niece
3. cousin
   son-in-law
4. sister-in-law
   brother-in-law

C. WHICH GROUP?
nephew   cousin   aunt
uncle   niece

D. WHO ARE THEY?
1. uncle
2. aunt
3. nephew
4. niece
5. father
6. aunt
7. uncle
8. sister

WORKBOOK PAGES 8–9

A. MATCHING
1. take a shower
2. comb my hair
3. go to bed
4. brush my teeth
5. get up
6. take a bath

B. WHAT DO YOU DO EVERY DAY?
1. make
2. brush
3. wash
4. eat
5. shave
6. sleep

C. LISTENING
Listen. Write the correct number.
1. (Sound: bath)
2. (Sound: shower)
3. (Sound: making dinner)
4. (Sound: brushing teeth)
5. (Sound: electric shaver)

Answers
2   3
4   5
1

WORKBOOK PAGES 10–11

A. LISTENING
Listen. Put a check under the correct picture.
1. A. What's John doing?
   B. He's sweeping the floor.
   A. Sweeping the floor?
   B. Yes.
2. A. What's Carol doing?
   B. She's ironing.
   A. Ironing?
   B. Yes.
3. A. What's Maria doing?
   B. She's listening to the radio.
   A. Listening to the radio?
   B. Yes.
4. A. What's your brother doing?
   B. He's washing the dishes.
   A. Washing the dishes?
   B. Yes.

5. A. What's Peter doing?
   B. He's doing the laundry.
   A. Doing the laundry?
   B. Yes.

6. A. What's your cousin doing?
   B. She's feeding the baby.
   A. Feeding the baby?
   B. Yes.

Answers
1. ✓ ___   2. ___ ✓
3. ___ ✓   4. ✓ ___
5. ✓ ___   6. ___ ✓

B. MATCHING
1. the dishes   3. TV
2. basketball   4. the cat

C. WHAT DO YOU DO EVERY DAY?
1. study   2. watch TV   3. dust
4. exercise   5. play   6. vacuum

D. LISTENING
Listen. Write the correct number.
1. (Sound: exercising/counting)
2. (Sound: basketball bouncing)
3. (Sound: broom sweeping floor)
4. (Sound: washing machine)
5. (Sound: washing dishes)
6. (Sound: vacuum cleaner)

Answers
3   5
6   4
1   2

WORKBOOK PAGES 12–13

A. WHAT'S THE WORD?
a. clock   f. desk
b. teacher   g. notebook
c. map   h. student
d. book   i. ruler
e. pencil   j. board

B. LISTENING
Listen and circle the word you hear.
1. A. Where's the pencil?
   B. The pencil? It's on the desk.
2. A. Where's the paper?
   B. The paper? It's on the bookshelf.
3. A. Where's the chalk?
   B. The chalk? It's on the teacher's desk.
4. A. Where's the ruler?
   B. The ruler? It's on my desk.
5. A. Where's your notebook?
   B. My notebook? It's in my desk.
6. A. Where's the computer?
   B. The computer? It's next to the TV.

Answers
1. pencil   4. ruler
2. paper   5. notebook
3. chalk   6. computer

C. WHAT'S IN THE CLASSROOM?
1. clock   4. map
2. globe   5. computer
3. book

WORKBOOK PAGES 14–15

A. LISTENING
Listen. Put a check under the correct picture.
1. A. Please write your name.
   B. Write my name? Sure.
2. A. Please close your book.
   B. Close my book? Sure.
3. A. Please help each other.
   B. Help each other? Okay.
4. A. Please stand up.
   B. Stand up? Okay.
5. A. Please put away your book.
   B. Put away my book? Okay.
6. A. Please raise your hand.
   B. Raise my hand? Okay.

Answers
1. ✓ ___   2. ___ ✓
3. ✓ ___   4. ✓ ___
5. ___ ✓   6. ___ ✓

B. MATCHING
1. up.   3. your book.
2. your name. 4. down.

C. WHAT'S THE ACTION?
1. Write   2. Go
3. Close   4. Give
5. Raise   6. Erase
7. Read   8. Work

WORKBOOK PAGES 16–17

A. LISTENING
Listen. Put a check under the correct picture.
1. A. Please do your homework.
   B. Do my homework? Okay.
2. A. Please check your answers.
   B. Check my answers? Okay.
3. A. Please watch the movie.
   B. Watch the movie? Okay.
4. A. Please hand in your homework.
   B. Hand in my homework? Okay.
5. A. Please answer the questions.
   B. Answer the questions? Okay.
6. A. Please turn off the lights.
   B. Turn off the lights? Okay.

Answers
1. ✓ ___   2. ___ ✓
3. ✓ ___   4. ✓ ___
5. ✓ ___   6. ___ ✓

B. MATCHING
1. the movie.   3. the lights.
2. your homework.   4. notes.

C. WHAT'S THE ACTION?

1. Check
2. Correct
3. Take
4. Watch
5. Answer
6. Do
7. Turn off
8. Lower

WORKBOOK PAGES 18–19

A. MATCHING

1. mobile home
2. farmhouse
3. dormitory
4. house
5. nursing home
6. cabin

B. CHOOSE THE CORRECT ANSWER

1. b
2. a
3. a
4. b

C. WHAT TYPE OF HOUSING?

1. cabin
2. trailer
3. house
4. farmhouse
5. apartment
6. shelter

WORKBOOK PAGES 20–21

A. CIRCLE THE CORRECT WORD

1. armchair
2. bookcase
3. rug
4. plant
5. floor
6. painting

B. WHERE IS IT?

1. lamp
2. picture
3. drapes
4. painting
5. pillow

C. WHAT'S THE WORD?

1. sofa
2. rug
3. lamp
4. window
5. bookcase
6. plant
7. television
8. fireplace
9. pillow

WORKBOOK PAGE 22

A. WHAT'S IN THE DINING ROOM?

1. candle
2. table
3. chair
4. pitcher
5. teapot

B. MATCHING

1. cabinet
2. shaker
3. dish
4. bowl
5. pot

C. LISTENING

Listen and circle the words you hear.

1. A. Please pass the butter dish.
   B. The butter dish? Here you are.
2. A. Please pass the pitcher.
   B. The pitcher? Here you are.
3. A. May I have the salt shaker, please?
   B. The salt shaker? Here you are.
4. A. I really like your tablecloth.
   B. My tablecloth? Thank you very much.
5. A. I really like your teapot.
   B. My teapot? Thank you very much.
6. A. I really like your sugar bowl.
   B. My sugar bowl? Thank you very much.

Answers

1. butter dish
2. pitcher
3. salt shaker
4. tablecloth
5. teapot
6. sugar bowl

WORKBOOK PAGE 23

A. CHOOSE THE CORRECT ANSWER

1. a
2. b
3. b
4. a

B. WHAT IS IT?

1. glass
2. cup
3. napkin
4. teaspoon
5. knife
6. fork

WORKBOOK PAGES 24–25

A. WHAT'S THE WORD?

1. pillow
2. bed
3. mirror
4. dresser
5. blanket
6. blinds

B. MATCHING

1. table
2. clock
3. box
4. bed
5. radio
6. spring

C. WHERE IS IT?

1. nightstand
2. bed
3. dresser
4. chest
5. mirror
6. blinds

D. LISTENING

Listen and circle the words you hear.

1. A. Ooh! There's a big bug on the blanket.
   B. On the blanket? I'll get it.
2. A. Ooh! There's a big bug on the dresser.
   B. On the dresser? I'll get it.
3. A. Ooh! There's a big bug on the bedspread.
   B. On the bedspread? I'll get it.
4. A. Excuse me. I'm looking for a mirror.
   B. Mirrors are over there.
   A. Thank you.
5. A. Excuse me. I'm looking for a pillow.
   B. Pillows are over there.
   A. Thank you.
6. A. Excuse me. I'm looking for a clock radio.
   B. Clock radios are over there.
   A. Thank you.

Answers

1. blanket
2. dresser
3. bedspread
4. mirror
5. pillow
6. clock radio

WORKBOOK PAGES 26–27

A. WHAT'S IN THE KITCHEN?

1. dishwasher
2. oven
3. toaster
4. cabinet
5. sink
6. stove
7. microwave
8. sponge
9. refrigerator

B. WHICH GROUP?

For cooking:
microwave
range

For cleaning:
dishwasher
sink

C. MATCHING

1. pail
2. opener
3. rack
4. board
5. chair
6. maker

D. WORDSEARCH (see p. 122)

WORKBOOK PAGE 28

A. WHAT IS IT?

1. stroller
2. crib
3. doll
4. car seat
5. swing
6. high chair

B. MATCHING

1. in the toy chest.
2. in the crib.
3. on the chest.
4. in the playpen.
5. next to the changing table.

WORKBOOK PAGE 29

A. WHAT IS IT?

1. ointment
2. bottle
3. nipple
4. bib
5. pacifier
6. baby food

B. MATCHING

1. powder
2. pins
3. ring
4. swabs
5. diapers

C. LISTENING

Listen. Write the number under the correct picture.

1. A. Where's the ointment?
   B. The ointment? It's on the changing table.
2. A. Where are the baby wipes?
   B. The baby wipes? They're on the changing table.
3. A. Where are the diaper pins?
   B. The diaper pins? They're on the changing table.
4. A. Where's the pacifier?
   B. The pacifier? It's in the crib.
5. A. Where's the bib?
   B. The bib? It's in the kitchen.
6. A. Where's the baby shampoo?
   B. The baby shampoo? It's on the changing table.

Answers

2	6	1	4	3	5

WORKBOOK PAGE 30

A. WHAT'S IN THE BATHROOM?

1. plunger
2. toothbrush
3. mirror
4. bathtub
5. sink
6. soap
7. shower
8. toilet
9. bath mat

B. LISTENING

Listen and circle the word you hear.

1. A. Did you clean the mirror?
   B. The mirror? No, not yet.
2. A. Did you clean the sink?
   B. The sink? No, not yet.
3. A. Did you clean the shower?
   B. The shower? No, not yet.
4. A. Did you clean the toilet?
   B. The toilet? No, not yet.
5. A. Did you clean the sponge?
   B. The sponge? No, not yet.
6. A. Did you clean the tub?
   B. The tub? No, not yet.

Answers

1. mirror
2. sink
3. shower
4. toilet
5. sponge
6. tub

WORKBOOK PAGE 31

A. WHAT IS IT?

1. comb
2. razor
3. toothbrush
4. shampoo
5. scissors
6. hair brush

B. WHICH GROUP?

For teeth:	For hair:
dental floss	brush
mouthwash	comb
toothbrush	conditioner
toothpaste	shampoo

C. LISTENING

Listen. Write the correct number.

1. A. Excuse me. Where can I find a hair brush?
   B. Hair brushes are in the next aisle.
   A. Thank you.
2. A. Excuse me. Where can I find shampoo?
   B. Shampoo is in the next aisle.
   A. Thank you.
3. A. Excuse me. Where can I find a comb?
   B. Combs are in the next aisle.
   A. Thank you.
4. A. Excuse me. Where can I find powder?
   B. Powder is over there.
   A. Thanks.
5. A. Excuse me. Where can I find toothpaste?
   B. Toothpaste is over there.
   A. Thanks.
6. A. Excuse me. Where can I find scissors?
   B. Scissors are in the next aisle.
   A. Thanks.

Answers

3	6	2
4	1	5

WORKBOOK PAGE 32

A. WHAT IS IT?

1. broom
2. mop
3. dustpan
4. iron
5. sponge
6. bucket

B. MATCHING

1. next to the dryer.
2. next to the dustpan.
3. next to the utility sink.
4. on the clothesline.
5. in the bucket.

C. LISTENING

Listen and circle the words you hear.

1. A. Excuse me. I'm looking for a broom.
   B. A broom? Brooms are at the back of the store.
2. A. Excuse me. I'm looking for an iron.
   B. An iron? We have irons at the back of the store.
3. A. Excuse me. I'm looking for a dustpan.
   B. A dustpan? We have dustpans at the back of the store.

4. A. Excuse me. I'm looking for clothespins.
   B. Clothespins? They're at the back of the store.
5. A. Excuse me. I'm looking for a bucket.
   B. Buckets are at the back of the store.
6. A. Excuse me. I'm looking for a sponge.
   B. Sponges are at the back of the store.

Answers
1. broom
2. iron
3. dustpan
4. clothespins
5. bucket
6. sponge

WORKBOOK PAGE 33

A. WHAT IS IT?
1. mailbox
2. garage
3. lamppost
4. lawnmower
5. window
6. chimney

B. MATCHING
1. door
2. mailbox
3. TV antenna
4. lawnmower
5. garage

WORKBOOK PAGE 34

A. CHOOSE THE CORRECT WORD
1. fire alarm
2. buzzer
3. elevator
4. balcony
5. laundry room
6. parking lot

B. MATCHING
1. room
2. pool
3. lot
4. detector
5. chute
6. conditioner

WORKBOOK PAGE 35

A. WHO IS IT?
1. locksmith
2. painter
3. carpenter
4. plumber
5. gardener
6. electrician

B. MATCHING: WHO REPAIRS IT?
1. TV repair person
2. plumber
3. carpenter
4. electrician
5. locksmith

WORKBOOK PAGE 36

A. WHAT IS IT?
1. saw
2. hammer
3. pliers
4. wrench
5. drill
6. screwdriver
7. hose
8. rake
9. shovel

B. LISTENING
Listen. Write the correct number.
1. (Sound: electric drill)
2. (Sound: hammer)
3. (Sound: lawnmower)
4. (Sound: sandpaper)
5. (Sound: saw)
6. (Sound: shovel)

Answers

2	4
5	1
6	3

WORKBOOK PAGES 37–38

A. MATCHING
1. three   3
2. eight   8
3. seven   7
4. one   1
5. six   6
6. four   4
7. two   2
8. ten   10
9. five   5
10. nine   9

B. WHAT'S THE NUMBER?
1. 7
2. 9
3. 2
4. 10
5. 8
6. 50
7. 30
8. 100
9. 21
10. 62

C. WHAT'S THE WORD?

three	fifteen
one	eleven
five	twelve
four	twenty-two
twenty	thirty-six

D. LISTENING
Listen and circle the number you hear.
1. A. How old is your daughter?
   B. She's thirteen years old.
   A. Thirteen?
   B. Yes.
2. A. How old is your son?
   B. He's forty years old.
   A. Forty?
   B. Yes.
3. A. How old is your brother?
   B. He's nineteen years old.
   A. Nineteen?
   B. Yes.
4. A. How old is your sister?
   B. She's eight years old.
   A. Eight?
   B. Yes.
5. A. How old is he?
   B. He's seventy years old.
   A. Seventy?
   B. Yes.
6. A. How old is she?
   B. She's sixteen years old.
   A. Sixteen?
   B. Yes.
7. A. How old are you?
   B. I'm twenty-four years old.
   A. Twenty-four?
   B. Yes.
8. A. How old are you?
   B. I'm thirty-five years old.
   A. Thirty-five?
   B. Yes.

1. 13
2. 40
3. 19
4. 8
5. 70
6. 16
7. 24
8. 35

WORKBOOK PAGE 39

A. MATCHING

1. 3rd
2. 9th
3. 1st
4. 12th
5. 60th
6. 11th
7. 8th
8. 4th
9. 80th
10. 14th

B. WHAT'S THE NUMBER?

1. 2nd
2. 10th
3. 13th
4. 1st
5. 50th

C. WHAT'S THE WORD?

fourteenth
sixth
sixtieth
eleventh
twentieth

D. MATCHING

1. fourth
2. fifth
3. second
4. first
5. third
6. tenth

E. LISTENING

Listen and circle the number you hear.

1. A. What floor do you live on?
   B. I live on the fourteenth floor.
   A. The fourteenth?
   B. Yes.
2. A. What floor do you live on?
   B. I live on the seventh floor.
   A. The seventh?
   B. Yes.
3. A. What floor do you live on?
   B. I live on the thirtieth floor.
   A. The thirtieth?
   B. Yes.
4. A. What floor do you live on?
   B. The eighteenth floor.
   A. The eighteenth?
   B. Yes.
5. A. What floor do you live on?
   B. The twenty-second floor.
   A. The twenty-second?
   B. Yes.

Answers

1. 14th
2. 7th
3. 30th
4. 18th
5. 22nd

WORKBOOK PAGES 40–41

A. MATCHING

1. multiplication
2. division
3. subtraction
4. addition

B. MATCHING

1. −
2. x
3. =
4. +
5. ÷

C. LISTENING

Listen and circle the answer.

1. A. How much is three times two?
   B. Three times two equals six.
2. A. How much is four plus five?
   B. Four plus five equals nine.
3. A. How much is nine divided by three?
   B. Nine divided by three equals three.
4. A. How much is eight minus two?
   B. Eight minus two equals six.
5. A. How much is two times five?
   B. Two times five equals ten.

Answers

1. x
2. +
3. ÷
4. −
5. x

D. WRITE THE MATH PROBLEMS

1. $\begin{array}{r} 1 \\ +3 \\ \hline 4 \end{array}$
2. $8 \div 4 = 2$
3. $2 \times 5 = 10$
4. $\begin{array}{r} 12 \\ -7 \\ \hline 5 \end{array}$

E. WHAT'S THE FRACTION?

1/4   1/2   1/3   2/3   3/4

F. MATCHING

1. 1/2
2. 1/4
3. 2/3
4. 3/4
5. 1/3

G. LISTENING

Listen and circle the answer.

1. A. Is this on sale?
   B. Yes. It's one third off the regular price.
   A. One third off the regular price?
   B. That's right.
2. A. Is this on sale?
   B. Yes. It's one half off the regular price.
   A. One half off the regular price?
   B. That's right.
3. A. Is this on sale?
   B. Yes. It's one quarter off the regular price.
   A. One quarter off the regular price?
   B. That's right.
4. A. The gas tank is three quarters full.
   B. Three quarters?
   A. Yes.
5. A. The gas tank is half full.
   B. Half full?
   A. Yes.

Answers

1. 1/3
2. 1/2
3. 1/4
4. 3/4
5. 1/2

H. WHAT'S THE PERCENT?

75%	25%	50%	100%

I. MATCHING

1. 50%
2. 25%
3. 100%
4. 30%
5. 75%

J. LISTENING

Listen and write the percent you hear.

1. A. There's a fifty percent chance of rain.
    B. Fifty percent?
    A. Yes.
2. A. There's a one hundred percent chance of
        rain.
    B. One hundred percent?
    A. Yes.
3. A. How did you do on the test?
    B. I got ninety percent of the answers right.
    A. Ninety percent?
    B. Yes.
4. A. How did you do on the test?
    B. I got seventy-five percent of the answers
        right.
    A. Seventy-five percent?
    B. Yes.
5. A. Is this on sale?
    B. Yes. It's twenty-five percent off the regular
        price.
    A. Twenty-five percent?
    B. Yes. That's right.
6. A. Is this on sale?
    B. Yes. It's ten percent off the regular price.
    A. Ten percent?
    B. Yes. That's right.

Answers

1. 50%
2. 100%
3. 90%
4. 75%
5. 25%
6. 10%

WORKBOOK PAGES 42–43

A. WHAT TIME IS IT?

8:00	2:15	6:45	4:30
5:05	10:20	12:55	6:40

B. CHOOSE THE CORRECT ANSWER

1. a
2. b
3. a
4. b

C. MATCHING

1. 3:45   three forty-five
2. 4:20   twenty after four
3. 4:30   four thirty
4. 4:15   four fifteen
5. 4:50   ten to five

D. CHOOSE THE CORRECT TIME

1. 7:00 A.M.
2. midnight
3. noon
4. 10:00 P.M.

E. LISTENING

Listen and circle the time you hear.

1. A. What time does the train leave?
    B. At eight thirty.
    A. Eight thirty? Thanks.
2. A. What time does the train leave?
    B. At ten o'clock.
    A. Ten o'clock? Thanks.
3. A. When does the bus leave?
    B. At three fifteen.
    A. Three fifteen? Thanks.
4. A. When does the bus leave?
    B. At six forty-five.
    A. Six forty-five? Thanks.
5. A. When will we arrive?
    B. At half past one.
    A. Half past one? Thanks.
6. A. When will we arrive?
    B. At one oh five.
    A. One oh five? Thanks.

Answers

1. 8:30
2. 10:00
3. 3:15
4. 6:45
5. 1:30
6. 1:05

WORKBOOK PAGES 44–45

A. WHAT'S MISSING?

1. January
2. February
3. March
4. April
5. May
6. June
7. July
8. August
9. September
10. October
11. November
12. December

B. WRITE THE MONTH

1. February
2. May
3. July
4. September
5. December

C. WHAT'S MISSING?

1. Sunday
2. Monday
3. Tuesday
4. Wednesday
5. Thursday
6. Friday
7. Saturday

D. WRITE THE DAY

1. Sunday
2. Monday
3. Tuesday
4. Wednesday
5. Thursday
6. Friday
7. Saturday

E. MATCHING

1. July 10, 1998
2. May 8, 1999
3. January 2, 1999
4. February 1, 1999
5. March 6, 1997

G. LISTENING

Listen and circle the correct answer.

1. A. What day is it?
    B. It's Monday.
    A. Monday? Thanks.

2. A. What day is it?
   B. Tuesday.
   A. Tuesday? Thanks.
3. A. What month is it?
   B. June.
   A. June? Thanks.
4. A. What month is it?
   B. It's December.
   A. December? Thanks.
5. A. What's today's date?
   B. Today is April fourth.
   A. April fourth? Thanks.
6. A. When is your birthday?
   B. My birthday is on March seventh.
   A. March seventh?
   B. Yes.

Answers
1. Monday   4. December
2. Tuesday   5. April 4
3. June   6. March 7

WORKBOOK PAGE 46

A. WHAT'S THE PLACE?
1. clinic   4. bus station
2. bakery   5. coffee shop
3. bank   6. book store

B. MATCHING
1. bakery   4. cafeteria
2. bank   5. cleaners
3. barber shop

WORKBOOK PAGE 47

A. WHAT'S THE PLACE?
1. grocery store   4. gas station
2. hair salon   5. hardware store
3. drug store   6. hospital

B. MATCHING
1. hardware store 4. gas station
2. drug store   5. florist
3. grocery store

WORKBOOK PAGE 48

A. WHAT'S THE PLACE?
1. museum   2. park   3. library
4. laundromat 5. pet shop   6. parking lot

B. WORDSEARCH (see p. 122)

WORKBOOK PAGE 49

A. WHAT'S THE PLACE?
1. school   4. zoo
2. restaurant   5. supermarket
3. post office   6. shopping mall

B. MATCHING
1. supermarket   4. restaurant
2. post office   5. train station
3. school

WORKBOOK PAGE 50

A. WHAT'S THE WORD?
1. meter maid   3. bus
2. meter   4. bus stop

5. taxi   7. sidewalk
6. taxi driver   8. street

B. YES OR NO?
1. No   4. No
2. Yes   5. Yes
3. Yes

WORKBOOK PAGE 51

A. WHAT'S THE WORD?
1. pedestrian   4. traffic light
2. crosswalk   5. street sign
3. police officer 6. intersection

B. MATCHING
1. light   4. officer
2. booth   5. truck
3. stand

C. WHICH GROUP?
People: Places:
pedestrian   intersection
police officer   fire station
street vendor   taxi stand

WORKBOOK PAGES 52–53

A. WHAT'S THE WORD?
1. new   3. tall   5. loose
2. old   4. short   6. tight

7. high   9. hot   11. large
8. low   10. cold   12. small

B. MATCHING: OPPOSITES
1. slow   6. narrow
2. little   7. young
3. light   8. bad
4. low   9. light
5. tight   10. cold

C. WHAT'S THE WORD?
1. short   2. small
3. narrow   4. cold
5. curly   6. heavy
7. new   8. young

WORKBOOK PAGES 54–55

A. WHAT'S THE WORD?
1. dry   3. fancy   5. empty
2. wet   4. plain   6. full

7. open   9. clean   11. neat
8. closed 10. dirty 12. messy

B. MATCHING: OPPOSITES
1. dirty   6. hard
2. difficult   7. ugly
3. plain   8. poor
4. married   9. dull
5. cheap   10. rough

C. WHAT'S THE WORD?
1. easy
2. single
3. closed
4. dry
5. plain
6. clean
7. dull
8. soft

WORKBOOK PAGE 56

A. LISTENING
Listen. Put a check under the correct picture.
1. A. You look sad.
   B. I am. I'm VERY sad.
2. A. You look cold.
   B. I am. I'm VERY cold.
3. A. You look thirsty.
   B. I am. I'm VERY thirsty.
4. A. You look sick.
   B. I am. I'm VERY sick.
5. A. Are you disappointed?
   B. Yes. I'm VERY disappointed.
6. A. Are you happy?
   B. Yes. I'm VERY happy.

Answers
1. ___ ✓
2. ✓ ___
3. ✓ ___
4. ___ ✓
5. ___ ✓
6. ✓ ___

B. WHAT'S THE WORD?
1. sad
2. cold
3. thirsty
4. sick
5. hot
6. happy

WORKBOOK PAGE 57

A. CHOOSE THE CORRECT WORD
1. proud
2. disgusted
3. worried
4. embarrassed
5. nervous
6. jealous

B. LISTENING
Listen. Write the number under the correct picture.
1. A. You look bored.
   B. I am. I'm VERY bored.
2. A. You look confused.
   B. I am. I'm VERY confused.
3. A. You look surprised.
   B. I am. I'm VERY surprised.
4. A. Are you nervous?
   B. Yes. I'm VERY nervous.
5. A. Are you proud?
   B. Yes. I'm VERY proud.
6. A. Are you angry?
   B. Yes. I'm VERY angry.

Answers
6   3   4   1   5   2

WORKBOOK PAGE 58

A. WHAT'S THE WORD?
1. lemon
2. pear
3. apple
4. plum
5. lime
6. banana
7. orange
8. peach
9. grapes

B. LISTENING
Listen and circle the fruit you hear.
1. A. How do you like the cherries?
   B. The cherries are delicious.
2. A. How do you like the lemons?
   B. The lemons are delicious.
3. A. How do you like the prunes?
   B. The prunes are delicious.
4. A. How do you like the papaya?
   B. The papaya is delicious.
5. A. How do you like the grapes?
   B. The grapes are delicious.
6. A. How do you like the tangerine?
   B. The tangerine is delicious.

Answers
1. cherries
4. papaya
2. lemons
5. grapes
3. prunes
6. tangerine

WORKBOOK PAGE 59

A. WHAT'S THE WORD?
1. onion
2. tomato
3. carrot
4. lettuce
5. radish
6. mushroom
7. corn
8. potato
9. cucumber

B. MATCHING
1. squash
4. bean
2. pepper
5. sprout
3. potato

WORKBOOK PAGE 60

A. WHAT'S THE WORD?
1. milk
2. cheese
3. butter
4. cream
5. eggs
6. yogurt
7. orange juice
8. cream cheese
9. sour cream
10. cottage cheese

WORKBOOK PAGES 61–62

A. WHAT'S THE WORD?
1. ketchup
2. juice
3. rice
4. bread
5. soda
6. mayonnaise
7. cereal
8. cookies
9. spaghetti
10. salt
11. soup
12. flour

B. MATCHING
1. paper
4. cream
2. sauce
5. towels
3. dressing

C. WHAT'S THE WORD?
1. rolls
2. soap
3. mustard
4. napkins
5. cake
6. ice cream
7. coffee
8. oil
9. pepper

WORKBOOK PAGE 63

A. CHOOSE THE CORRECT WORD
1. lamb
2. turkey
3. ground beef
4. crabs
5. pork
6. shrimp

B. WHAT'S THE WORD?

1. fish	2. chicken	3. steak
4. ham	5. bacon	6. lobster

WORKBOOK PAGE 64

A. CHOOSE THE CORRECT WORD

1. cashier	2. aisle	3. packer
4. cash register	5. paper bag	6. scale
7. shopping cart	8. shopping basket	

B. WHICH GROUP?

People:	Things:
bagger	counter
cashier	paper bag
shopper	scale

WORKBOOK PAGE 65

A. WHAT'S THE WORD?

1. dozen	4. bunch
2. can	5. box
3. bag	6. bar

B. MATCHING

1. soap	5. soup
2. cereal	6. eggs
3. ketchup	7. cottage cheese
4. bananas	

WORKBOOK PAGE 66

A. WHAT'S THE WORD?

1. pint	4. pound
2. quart	5. liter
3. loaf	6. gallon

B. MATCHING

1. mustard	5. orange juice
2. bread	6. sour cream
3. rolls	7. paper towels
4. apples	

WORKBOOK PAGE 67

A. CHOOSE THE CORRECT WORD

1. slice	2. bake	3. grate
4. fry	5. pour	6. beat

B. MATCHING

1. the onions.	4. the eggs.
2. the potatoes.	5. the vegetables.
3. the orange.	

WORKBOOK PAGE 68

A. WHAT'S THE WORD?

1. muffin	2. bagel	3. lemonade
4. coffee	5. donut	6. hamburger
7. hot dog	8. tea	9. milk

B. WHICH GROUP?

eat:		drink:	
taco	hot dog	coffee	milk
donut	hamburger	lemonade	tea

C. LISTENING

Listen. Write the number under the correct picture.

1. A. May I help you?
   B. Yes. I'd like a cheeseburger, please.
   A. A cheeseburger?
   B. Yes.
2. A. May I help you?
   B. Yes. I'd like a slice of pizza, please.
   A. A slice of pizza?
   B. Yes.
3. A. May I help you?
   B. Yes. I'd like a sandwich, please.
   A. A sandwich?
   B. Yes.
4. A. May I help you?
   B. Yes. I'd like a taco, please.
   A. A taco?
   B. Yes.
5. A. May I help you?
   B. Yes. I'd like a hot dog, please.
   A. A hot dog?
   B. Yes.
6. A. May I help you?
   B. Yes. I'd like an iced tea, please.
   A. An iced tea?
   B. Yes.

Answers

3	5	1	6	4	2

WORKBOOK PAGE 69

A. WHAT'S THE WORD?

1. booth	2. waitress	3. dishwasher
4. cashier	5. cook	6. high chair
7. waiter	8. table	9. menu

B. LISTENING

Listen. Write the number under the correct picture.

1. A. Do you have any job openings?
   B. Yes. We're looking for a busboy.
   A. A busboy?
   B. Yes.
2. A. Do you have any job openings?
   B. Yes. We're looking for a waitress.
   A. A waitress?
   B. Yes.
3. A. Do you have any job openings?
   B. Yes. We're looking for a dishwasher.
   A. A dishwasher?
   B. Yes.
4. A. Do you have any job openings?
   B. Yes. We're looking for a cashier.
   A. A cashier?
   B. Yes.
5. A. Do you have any job openings?
   B. Yes. We're looking for a cook.
   A. A cook?
   B. Yes.

6. A. Do you have any job openings?
   B. Yes. We're looking for a waiter.
   A. A waiter?
   B. Yes.

Answers

5   2   6   1   4   3

WORKBOOK PAGE 70

A. WHAT'S THE COLOR?

1. red
2. blue
3. brown
4. green
5. yellow
6. pink
7. orange
8. black
9. white

B. CROSSWORD (see p. 122)

WORKBOOK PAGE 71

A. WHAT'S THE WORD?

1. shirt
2. suit
3. blouse
4. jacket
5. pants
6. skirt
7. sweater
8. dress
9. shorts

B. LISTENING

Listen and circle the word you hear.

1. A. Do you like my new blouse?
   B. Yes. It's a very nice blouse.
2. A. Do you like my new jacket?
   B. Yes. It's a very nice jacket.
3. A. Do you like my new shirt?
   B. Yes. It's a very nice shirt.
4. A. Do you like my new tie?
   B. Yes. It's a very nice tie.
5. A. Do you like my new suit?
   B. Yes. It's a very nice suit.
6. A. Do you like my new skirt?
   B. Yes. It's a very nice skirt.

Answers

1. blouse
4. tie
2. jacket
5. suit
3. shirt
6. skirt

WORKBOOK PAGE 72

A. WHAT'S THE WORD?

1. stockings
2. pajamas
3. shoes
4. socks
5. bathrobe
6. boots
7. sneakers
8. sandals
9. nightgown

B. WHICH GROUP?

Sleepwear:	Underwear:	Footwear:
nightgown	briefs	boots
pajamas	undershirt	shoes

WORKBOOK PAGE 73

A. WHAT'S THE WORD?

1. rubbers
2. jacket
3. hat
4. poncho
5. raincoat
6. gloves
7. coat
8. mittens
9. swimsuit

B. WHICH GROUP?

It's raining!	It's cold!
poncho	coat
raincoat	gloves
rubbers	scarf

WORKBOOK PAGE 74

A. CHOOSE THE CORRECT WORD

1. earrings
2. necklace
3. umbrella
4. watch
5. backpack
6. ring

B. MATCHING

1. band
4. links
2. purse
5. ring
3. bag

WORKBOOK PAGE 75

A. WHAT'S THE WORD?

1. tight
3. small
5. light
2. loose
4. large
6. heavy

7. short
9. plain
11. low
8. long
10. fancy
12. high

B. MATCHING: OPPOSITES

1. short
4. plain
2. light
5. narrow
3. baggy

WORKBOOK PAGE 76

A. WHAT IS IT?

1. nickel   2. penny   3. quarter
   5¢ $.05   1¢ $.01   25¢ $.25
4. half dollar   5. dime
   50¢ $.50   10¢ $.10

B. WHAT'S THE AMOUNT?

1. $.05
2. $.15
3. $.30
4. $.12
5. $.26
6. $.25
7. $.75
8. $1.00

WORKBOOK PAGE 77

A. MATCHING

1. ten dollars $10.00
2. one dollar $1.00
3. fifty dollars $50.00
4. five dollars $5.00
5. twenty dollars $20.00

B. WHAT'S THE AMOUNT?

1. $11.00   2. $15.00
3. $30.00   4. $10.00

C. LISTENING

Listen and circle the amount you hear.

1. A. How much is this?
   B. Thirty-five dollars.
   A. Thirty-five dollars?
   B. Yes.
2. A. How much is this?
   B. Five dollars.
   A. Five dollars?
   B. Yes.

3. A. How much is this?
   B. Forty-four cents.
   A. Forty-four cents?
   B. Yes.
4. A. How much is this?
   B. Sixty-one dollars.
   A. Sixty-one dollars?
   B. Yes.
5. A. How much is this?
   B. Seven dollars and ten cents.
   A. Seven dollars and ten cents?
   B. Yes.
6. A. How much is this?
   B. Forty-one dollars and fourteen cents.
   A. Forty-one dollars and fourteen cents?
   B. Yes.

Answers

1. $35.00	4. $61.00
2. $5.00	5. $7.10
3. $.44	6. $41.14

WORKBOOK PAGES 78–79

A. CHOOSE THE CORRECT WORD

1. check	2. credit card	3. money order
4. deposit slip	5. bank book	6. teller

C. AT THE BANK

(Students should write correct date, account number, and amount on each bank slip. They should also put their signature on #1 and #2.)

WORKBOOK PAGE 80

A. WHAT IS IT?

a. head	i. neck
b. hair	j. shoulder
c. eye	k. chest
d. ear	l. back
e. nose	m. arm
f. mouth	n. elbow
g. teeth	o. waist
h. chin	p. leg

WORKBOOK PAGE 81

A. WHAT IS IT?

a. hand	c. thumb	e. ankle
b. finger	d. foot	f. toe

B. MATCHING: WHERE ARE THEY?

1. toe	4. head
2. hand	5. neck
3. foot	

C. HOW MANY DO WE HAVE?

1. 2	5. 10
2. 10	6. 1
3. 1	7. 2
4. 2	8. 1

WORKBOOK PAGE 82

A. CHOOSE THE CORRECT WORD

1. insect bite	2. headache	3. stomachache
4. fever	5. cough	6. toothache
7. cold	8. stiff neck	9. the chills

B. LISTENING

Listen and circle the word you hear.

1. A. What's the matter?
   B. I have a headache.
   A. A headache? I'm sorry to hear that.
2. A. What's the matter?
   B. I have a cold.
   A. A cold? I'm sorry to hear that.
3. A. What's the matter?
   B. I have a stomachache.
   A. A stomachache? I'm sorry to hear that.
4. A. What's the matter?
   B. I have a virus.
   A. A virus? I'm sorry to hear that.
5. A. What's the matter?
   B. I have a fever.
   A. A fever? I'm sorry to hear that.
6. A. What's the matter?
   B. I have the hiccups.
   A. The hiccups? I'm sorry to hear that.

Answers

1. headache	4. virus
2. cold	5. fever
3. stomachache	6. hiccups

WORKBOOK PAGE 83

A. CHOOSE THE CORRECT WORD

1. dizzy	2. burn	3. cut
4. exhausted	5. cough	6. sneeze

B. WORDSEARCH (see p. 123)

WORKBOOK PAGE 84

A. CHOOSE THE CORRECT WORD

1. dentist	2. pediatrician	3. X-ray technician
4. surgeon	5. optometrist	6. EMT
7. stethoscope	8. thermometer	9. scale

B. MATCHING

1. lab technician	4. cardiologist
2. dentist	5. pediatrician
3. optometrist	

WORKBOOK PAGE 85

A. CHOOSE THE CORRECT WORD

1. sling	2. injection	3. cast
4. exercise	5. surgery	6. stitches
7. I.V.	8. hospital bed	9. bandaid

B. MATCHING

1. therapy	4. pan
2. tests	5. gown
3. button	

WORKBOOK PAGE 86

A. CHOOSE THE CORRECT WORD
1. eye drops
2. aspirin
3. antacid tablets
4. vitamins
5. heating pad
6. cold tablets
7. capsule
8. pill
9. teaspoon

B. MATCHING
1. syrup
2. lozenges
3. spray
4. pad
5. tablets

WORKBOOK PAGE 87

A. WHAT'S THE WORD?
1. envelope
2. stamp
3. postcard
4. letter
5. package
6. mailbox
7. zip code
8. aerogramme
9. money order

B. MATCHING
1. carrier
2. address
3. mail
4. order
5. post
6. code

WORKBOOK PAGE 88

A. WHAT'S THE WORD?
1. librarian
2. checkout desk
3. shelves
4. card catalog
5. atlas
6. encyclopedia
7. newspaper
8. magazine

B. LISTENING

Listen and circle the words you hear.
1. A. Excuse me. Where's the card catalog?
   B. The card catalog? Over there.
   A. Thank you.
2. A. Excuse me. Where are the magazines?
   B. The magazines? Over there.
   A. Thank you.
3. A. Excuse me. Where's the librarian?
   B. The librarian? He's over there.
   A. Thank you.
4. A. Excuse me. Where are the dictionaries?
   B. The dictionaries? Over there.
   A. Thank you.
5. A. Excuse me. Where are the atlases?
   B. The atlases? Over there.
   A. Thank you.
6. A. Excuse me. Where's the information desk?
   B. The information desk? Over there.
   A. Thank you.

Answers
1. card catalog
2. magazines
3. librarian
4. dictionaries
5. atlases
6. information desk

WORKBOOK PAGE 89

A. WHERE ARE THEY?
1. principal, office
2. coach, gym
3. custodian, cafeteria
4. teacher, chemistry lab
5. guidance counselor, guidance office
6. school nurse, nurse's office

WORKBOOK PAGE 90

A. WHAT'S THE WORD?
1. health
2. history
3. Spanish
4. English
5. science
6. math
7. art
8. music
9. geography
10. driver's ed
11. home economics

WORKBOOK PAGE 91

A. WHAT'S THE WORD?
1. choir
2. drama
3. yearbook
4. band
5. orchestra
6. football
7. literary magazine
8. school newspaper
9. student government

WORKBOOK PAGE 92

A. WHAT'S THE OCCUPATION?
1. butcher
2. assembler
3. bricklayer
4. barber
5. cashier
6. accountant

B. MATCHING: WHO USES IT?
1. accountant
2. carpenter
3. artist
4. cashier
5. barber

WORKBOOK PAGE 93

A. WHAT'S THE OCCUPATION?
1. gardener
2. custodian
3. hairdresser
4. farmer
5. chef
6. housekeeper

B. MATCHING: WHO USES IT?
1. custodian
2. chef
3. construction worker
4. gardener
5. hairdresser

WORKBOOK PAGE 94

A. WHAT'S THE OCCUPATION?
1. pharmacist
2. plumber
3. salesperson
4. mechanic
5. painter
6. lawyer

B. WORDSEARCH (see p. 123)

WORKBOOK PAGE 95

A. WHAT'S THE OCCUPATION?
1. secretary
2. welder
3. scientist
4. waiter
5. waitress
6. stock clerk

B. CROSSWORD (see p. 123)

WORKBOOK PAGE 96

A. WHAT DO THEY DO?
1. cook
2. clean
3. deliver
4. drive
5. file
6. assemble

B. MATCHING
1. cook.
2. act.
3. drive.
4. mow lawns.
5. assemble components.
6. build things.
7. clean.

WORKBOOK PAGE 97

A. WHAT DO THEY DO?
1. paint
2. serve
3. sell
4. wash
5. type
6. repair

B. MATCHING
1. paints.
2. types.
3. serves food.
4. sews.
5. sells things.

WORKBOOK PAGE 98

A. CHOOSE THE CORRECT WORD
1. time clock
2. first-aid kit
3. cafeteria
4. forklift
5. conveyor belt
6. assembly line
7. safety glasses
8. hand truck
9. suggestion box

B. MATCHING
1. clock
2. line
3. station
4. kit
5. belt

WORKBOOK PAGE 99

A. WHAT'S THE WORD?
1. helmet
2. ladder
3. bulldozer
4. cement
5. wire
6. dump truck
7. wood
8. brick
9. wheelbarrow

B. WHICH GROUP?

Materials:	Machines:
beam	backhoe
pipe	bulldozer
plywood	cement mixer

WORKBOOK PAGE 100

A. WHAT'S THE WORD?
1. battery
2. engine
3. radiator
4. tire
5. headlight
6. bumper
7. gas station
8. gas pump
9. mechanic
10. flare
11. jack
12. spare tire

B. MATCHING
1. wipers
2. defroster
3. plate
4. plugs
5. belt

WORKBOOK PAGE 101

A. CHOOSE THE CORRECT WORD
1. seat belt
2. steering column
3. accelerator
4. gearshift
5. speedometer
6. rearview mirror
7. radio
8. air bag
9. turn signal

B. MATCHING
1. bag
2. belt
3. mirror
4. signal
5. brake

WORKBOOK PAGE 102

A. WHAT'S THE WORD?
1. bus
2. taxi
3. bus station
4. conductor
5. luggage
6. train
7. bus driver
8. bus stop
9. subway

B. MATCHING
1. car
2. driver
3. counter
4. card
5. station

WORKBOOK PAGE 103

A. CHOOSE THE CORRECT WORD
1. suitcase
2. ticket
3. customs officer
4. passport
5. security guard
6. boarding pass
7. baggage claim area
8. metal detector

B. MATCHING
1. officer
2. guard
3. counter
4. pass
5. detector

WORKBOOK PAGES 104–105

A. WHAT'S THE WEATHER?
1. clear
2. snowing
3. foggy
4. sunny
5. windy
6. raining
7. cloudy
8. humid
9. lightning

B. WHAT'S THE SEASON?
1. winter
2. spring
3. fall
4. summer

C. CROSSWORD (see p. 124)

WORKBOOK PAGES 106–107

A. WHAT'S THE WORD?
1. skating
2. swimming
3. sailing
4. jogging
5. fishing
6. tennis
7. bicycling
8. baseball
9. basketball
10. soccer
11. football
12. skiing

B. CROSSWORD (see p. 124)

WORKBOOK PAGE 27

D. WORDSEARCH

WORKBOOK PAGE 48

B. WORDSEARCH

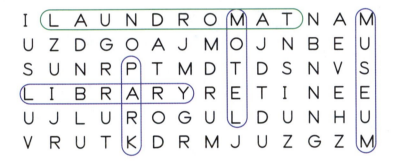

WORKBOOK PAGE 70

B. CROSSWORD

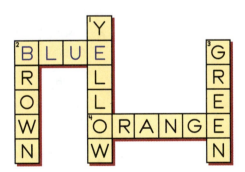

B. WORDSEARCH

WORKBOOK PAGE 94

B. WORDSEARCH

WORKBOOK PAGE 95

B. CROSSWORD

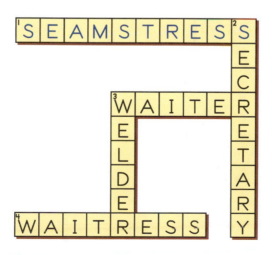

WORKBOOK PAGE 105

C. CROSSWORD

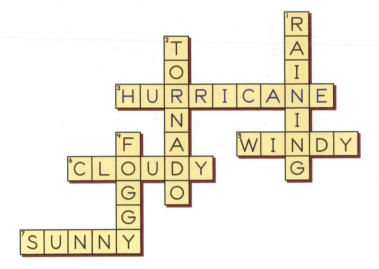

WORKBOOK PAGE 107

B. CROSSWORD

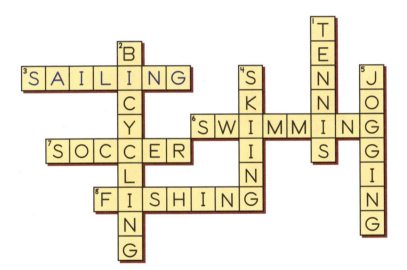